So You Think You Know

YOU KNOW

DR WHO?

Hodder
Children's
Books

A division of Hachette Children's Books

CONTENTS

Questions

Easy quiz   1

Medium quizzes   7

Difficult quiz   118

Answers

Easy quiz   124

Medium quizzes   125

Difficult quiz   140

INTRODUCTION

So you think you know all there is to know about *Doctor Who* – the Doctor's many foibles, companions, adventures and adversaries? You reckon you can summon up from deep memory all of the planets, gadgets, plots and conspiracies the mysterious Time Lord encountered on our television screens? Then this book is for you.

Contained within these pages are over 1,000 questions about the episodes and making of the famous BBC series, as well as a smattering about the 1996 TV movie starring Paul McGann. Be warned – some are as tough as a Sontaran guard and many are more fiendish than the Master's myriad schemes to take control of the universe.

ABOUT THE AUTHOR

As a very young boy, Clive Gifford hid behind the sofa as the distinctive *Doctor Who* theme music sounded on Saturday evenings. As a slightly older child, he was thrilled to see his name appear on the TV screen in the credits – although this was another, adult, Clive Gifford, who was in charge of studio sound for the show. That was the closest Clive ever got to *Doctor Who* stardom – although his mate's uncle, Yuri Gridneff, did play a walk-on Shrieve in *The Ribos Operation*, and Clive did talk with Christopher Eccleston when they both appeared at an Amnesty International charity night.

Clive is an award-winning writer of dozens of books for young people, including: *How The Future Began*, *The Cosmic Toaster*, *Pants Attack*, *Mr Martin's A Martian*, and other books in the *So You Think You Know . . .* series including *The Lord of the Rings*, *The Simpsons*, *Premier League Football* and *Harry Potter*. He lives in Manchester with his wife, Jane, and their cat, Reg.

EASY QUIZ

1. What is the abbreviated name of the machine the Doctor time-travels in?

2. The Doctor is a member of which group: the Sontarans, the Time Lords or the Masters?

3. Which Doctor drove an antique car: the second, third, fourth or fifth?

4. The transformation of the Doctor is described by which word, beginning with the letter R?

5. A new *Doctor Who* series began filming in 2004. Which actor plays the Doctor?

6. How many hearts does the Doctor have?

7. The Doctor was accompanied on a number of his adventures by a robot dog. What was its name?

8. Which actor played the Doctor first: Jon Pertwee or Tom Baker?

9. What is a Type 40 TT Capsule better known as?

10. In the 2004 series, the Doctor's companion is played by which pop singer?

11. What long and colourful item of clothing did the fourth Doctor wear?

12. The Doctor's time-travel machine looks like what object?

13. In August 2004, after several months of negotiations, it was announced that the Doctor's most popular adversaries would feature in the new series. Who are these adversaries?

14. Which actor, who became famous as Dirty Den in *EastEnders*, played Kiston in the story, *Resurrection of the Daleks*?

15. If you heard a metallic voice order: 'Exterminate!' which of Doctor Who's opponents would you be encountering?

16. Which actor played Doctor Who immediately before Colin Baker?

17. Which Doctor Who performed magic tricks in *The Greatest Show in the Galaxy*: the fifth Doctor, the sixth Doctor or the seventh Doctor?

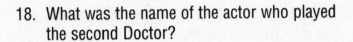

18. What was the name of the actor who played the second Doctor?

19. In *Revenge of the Cybermen*, which precious metal can kill the Cybermen?

20. Which of the third Doctor's companions was a journalist?

21. One of the first companions of the Doctor was played by which *Blue Peter* presenter?

22. Which frequent adversaries of the Doctor use a Time Destructor to age Sara Kingdom to death?

23. Is the TV series of the ninth Doctor filmed at: BBC Cardiff, BBC Manchester or BBC London?

24. From which solar system planet did the Ice Warriors come?

25. The first Doctor was forced to regenerate after battling which famous foe?

26. Where would you find the Death Zone: Earth, Venus, Skaro or Gallifrey?

27. Logopolis is home to a race of: warriors, mathematicians, nurses or spies?

28. Which famous children's puppeteer appeared as a follower of the Master in *Doctor Who*: Rod Hull, Roger De Courcey or Matthew Corbett?

29. Which of the following was not a feature of K-9: a nose-laser, articulated sensors or missile-firing tail?

30. Which Doctor's dress sense included velvet jackets and frilly-fronted shirts: the second Doctor, the third Doctor or the fourth Doctor?

31. What was the name of the first actor to play Doctor Who?

32. What Scottish musical instrument does Jamie discover in the TARDIS in *The Abominable Snowmen*?

33. Which *Carry On* star played an Ice Warrior in *The Ice Warriors*: Kenneth Williams, Sid James, Bernard Bresslaw or Kenneth Connor?

34. In *Frontier in Space*, which HG Wells novel is the Master seen reading?

35. In the 2004 series, what is the first name of the Doctor's female companion?

36. Which actor played the third Doctor Who?

37. In *The Myth Makers*, which Ancient Greek god is Doctor Who mistaken for?

38. Which female companion served with both the fifth and sixth Doctors?

39. *The Faceless Ones* starts with the TARDIS landing on a runway at which British airport?

40. Richard Hurndall took the place of which Doctor Who for the story, *The Five Doctors*?

41. Which major adversary of the Doctor's was played by Anthony Ainley?

42. What was the name of the seventh Doctor's last companion?

43. Which Doctor tried to strangle his own companion, Peri?

44. In *Full Circle*, does Adric injure his: knee, hand or chest?

45. What was the name of the actor who played the fifth Doctor?

46. In the story, *The Two Doctors*, what is the photographic name of the space station on which Androgums work?

47. Which actor played the Doctor in the story, *The Deadly Assassin*?

48. What colour is the ray from Davros's artificial eye in *Revelation of the Daleks*?

49. With what common poison did the sixth Doctor kill Shockeye?

50. Which Doctor was played by Sylvester McCoy: the fifth, sixth or seventh?

MEDIUM QUIZZES

QUIZ 1

1. Sharaz Jek becomes infatuated with which of the Doctor's companions?

2. Which one of the following stories did not feature the TARDIS: *The Wheel in Space*, *The Abominable Snowmen* or *Doctor Who and the Silurians*?

3. In *The Rescue*, Vicki adopts a Sand Beast. Is it vegetarian, is it a human-flesh eater or does it feed off the energy from brainwaves?

4. Who is the brother of Turlough: Malkon, Morgus or Sharaz Jek?

5. In *The Masque of Mandragora*, which one of the following things is not true about Hieronymous: he is the court astrologist, he is the leader of the cult of Demnos, he is the Master in disguise?

6. The first time a Dalek appeared in *Doctor Who*, we saw its arm menacing which person?

7. Before Ben Jackson became a companion of Doctor Who, he served in which military force?

8. In which story featuring the seventh Doctor was there a plot to kill Queen Victoria?

9. How many years had the Argolins been working on the science of Tachyonics?

10. What was the name of the composer of the original *Doctor Who* theme?

11. What was the name of the female replacement for the Doctor as UNIT's scientific advisor?

12. In *Planet of Evil*, which professor went insane after being infected with anti-matter?

13. In *The Happiness Patrol*, the Doctor uses what sort of food or drink to stick the Kandyman to the floor?

14. On what planet did the Doctor first encounter his companion, Ace?

15. Which former Minister of Justice has a time cabinet which works using zygma energy: the Master, Magnus Greel or the Monk?

16. A Doctor and his companion married in real life in 1980. Can you name the actors who played them?

17. In *Ghost Light*, a deranged Redvers Fenn-Cooper confronts the Doctor and Ace with a gun. But what weapon did he brandish first?

18. In *The Sontaran Experiment*, who removes the terulian diode bypasser from the Sontaran's ship: Harry, Sarah or the Doctor?

19. The First Elder is the leader of creatures which are telepathic and can control human minds. Are these creatures: Daleks, Sensorites, Thals or Sea Devils?

20. *Power of the Daleks* is set on which planet: Venus, Vulcan, Voord or Vofors Alpha?

21. What does the Kraal's planet, Oseidon, have the highest levels of in the known galaxy: oxygen, radiation, gold or cyanide?

22. In *The Curse of Peladon*, which *Doctor Who* companion kisses Peladon goodbye?

23. Brigadier Lethbridge-Stewart never appeared in a regular TV episode with which Doctor: the fifth, sixth or seventh?

24. In *The Web Planet*, Barbara works for the Zarbi on which planet?

25. Which character in the 2004 series of *Doctor Who* is played by Noel Clark?

26. The third Doctor was regenerated by an overdose of what?

27. In *The Daleks*, which was the warrior race on Skaro before the war: the Thals or the Daleks?

28. The director of the council which rules the planet, Dulkis, is: Senex, Rago or Toba?

29. In *Doctor Who: The Movie*, which enemy of the Doctor is finally sucked into the Eye of Harmony?

30. Can you remember either of Brigadier Lethbridge-Stewart's first names?

31. The Doctor's home planet was first named as Gallifrey in which *Doctor Who* story?

32. In *The Tenth Planet*, what was the name of the planet which was Earth's twin?

33. In which story is the Doctor caught up in the struggle for Pirate Avery's treasure?

34. Actress Carmen Silvera played three roles in *The Celestial Toymaker*. Which one of the following was not a role she played: Clara, Miss Wiggs, Ruth, Queen of Hearts?

35. In *Warriors of the Deep*, Commander Vorshak leads: Seabase Four, Seabase Fourteen or Seabase Forty?

36. In *The War Games*, which one of the following was not a triangular time zone: the American Civil War zone, the Hundred Years War zone, the Boer War zone or the Mexican Civil War zone?

37. What is the name of the village which features in the story, *The Daemons*?

38. *The Abominable Snowmen* featured a Tibetan warrior monk called Ralpachan. Ralpachan was acted by which notable British playwright?

39. Ace's home town was: Portsmouth, Perivale, Plymouth or Potters Bar?

40. Who or what commanded the robot Yeti?

41. In *Ghost Light*, Josiah Samuel Smith had a servant called: Namos, Nimrod, Nancy or Nicolai?

42. In *The Green Death*, the BOSS computer plans to devolve its power to how many international computers?

43. Which *Doctor Who* actor was also the tough sergeant in the first *Carry On* film, *Carry On Sergeant*?

44. In *Inferno*, Stahlman's Gas is drilled for on which planet?

45. In *The Five Doctors*, which one of the Doctors carried fireworks in their pocket?

46. Can you name two of the four *Doctor Who* stories which feature Borusa?

47. In *Invasion of the Dinosaurs*, the British government moves out of London to which Yorkshire town?

48. In the story, *Underworld*, what is the name, beginning with the letter O, of the computer on the P7E ship?

49. What device alters the size of the TARDIS and is first discussed in *The Wheel in Space*?

50. In which century is the *The Dalek Invasion of Earth* set: the twentieth, twenty-first, twenty-second or twenty-third?

1. Can you name the two female companions who served with the fourth and fifth Doctor?

2. In *The Crusade*, which *Doctor Who* companion was knighted by Richard the Lionheart?

3. In *Arc of Infinity*, Omega tried to recreate himself in which European city?

4. Who replaced Jo Grant as the third Doctor's companion?

5. Where is the Centre for Alien Biomorphology found: on Venus, on Antarctica, on an asteroid or on a space station orbiting Gallifrey?

6. What is the only 50 minute-long *Doctor Who* episode?

7. In which Daleks-based story did Doctor Who disguise himself as a Thal guard?

8. Which actor played the Doctor in more TV episodes than any other?

9. Who was originally a Time Lord like Doctor Who: Omega, Aggedor, Davros or the Brigadier?

10. Which one of the following was not a *Doctor Who* story: *The Two Doctors*, *The Three Doctors* or *The Four Doctors*?

11. In *Four to Doomsday*, who speaks and understands the Aboriginal language?

12. In *The Time Monster*, what is the name of the time-eating entity summoned by the Master?

13. In *The Claws of Axos*, from which country was Bill Filer sent as an agent to search for the Master?

14. How many cyberbombs are strapped to the Doctor when he is sent down to Voga?

15. Which computer hidden in the Post Office Tower can hypnotise people down a telephone line?

16. The Sontarans made their first appearance as an enemy of which Doctor: the second, third, fourth or fifth?

17. In *The Space Pirates*, what is the name of the pirates' leader: Dervish, Caven or Issigri?

18. In which story does the Doctor propose the building of the Trojan wooden horse?

19. Castrovalva is a trap set by which adversary of the Doctor?

20. In *The Macra Terror*, Officia is the colonist in charge of: the mine, the communications tower or the spaceport?

21. The hijacking of the TARDIS using a guidance system distorter damages which Doctor enough to force him to regenerate: the second Doctor, the fourth Doctor or the sixth Doctor?

22. By how many years does the Doctor age when he enters the Tachyon Recreation Generator?

23. With which Commander did Leela stay when she left the Doctor?

24. In *Terror of the Autons*, a Time Lord travels 29,000 light years to warn the Doctor of the arrival on Earth of which enemy?

25. Who persuaded Turlough to attempt to destroy the Doctor?

26. How many times did Doctor Who give a K-9 robot as a gift?

27. In a story featuring Romana and the fourth Doctor, what is the name of the giant squid which the Swampies worship?

28. Which Daleks-based story features a couple remaining on Earth in the year 2164?

29. *The Five Doctors* twentieth anniversary special was produced for which BBC charity event?

30. Which actress who played a *Doctor Who* companion married the science writer, Richard Dawkins, in 1992?

31. In *Planet of the Daleks*, the Daleks are on a mission to learn how to become invisible from which creatures, beginning with the letter S?

32. In *City of Death*, who is the last of the Jagaroth?

33. In *The Keys of Marinus*, who was the keeper of the conscience of Marinus: Arbitan, Vargos, Jano or Melkur?

34. The architect Kroagnon designed a building which the seventh Doctor and Mel visit to swim in its swimming pool. What is the building's name?

36. *Men Behaving Badly* star Martin Clunes appeared as Lon in: *Arc of Infinity, Snakedance* or *The Caves of Androzani*?

35. Who kisses the Doctor in *The Space Pirates*?

37. In *The Invasion of Time*, can you name either of the races of creatures which threaten Gallifrey?

38. Whose room inside the TARDIS becomes taken by Turlough?

39. In *The Ice Warriors*, Penley was played by an actor who found fame in *The Last of the Summer Wine* and as the voice of Wallace in *Wallace and Gromit*. Who was he?

40. In *Inside the Spaceship*, what heals the Doctor's injured head: a head regeneration unit, a Kroton spell or a magic bandage?

41. What is the name of the Royal Beast of Peladon, beginning with the letter A?

42. In *The Visitation*, who started the Great Fire of London in 1666?

43. One of Doctor Who's first companions in the 1960s was played by actress Jacqueline Hill. Who did she reappear as in the 1980s: Lexa, Vivas or Solon?

44. Does Vicki name the robotic servants of the Rills: Chumblies, Servos or Robo-Rills?

45. What colour were the question marks on the sweater worn by the seventh Doctor?

46. In *Trial of a Time Lord*, one character is known by three different names. Which of these is not one of them: Hallett, Enzu, Crawford or Grenville?

47. Which actor played the Doctor in *Fury from the Deep*?

48. The executive producer of the 2004 *Doctor Who* series is a famous TV writer of shows including *Queer As Folk* and *Bob and Rose* and *The Second Coming*. Who is he?

49. The Axons brought to Earth an allegedly limitless supply of energy. What was this called.

50. In which third Doctor story would you see General Carrington stuck to a vintage car when the Doctor presses his anti-theft switch?

1. In *The Ark in Space*, what is the real name of the commander of the ark: Lazar, Noah, Vural or Zake?

2. What poison does the Doctor place in the ventilation system of Solon's laboratory to kill Solon?

3. The Great Seal of Diplos turns out to be which segment of the Key to Time: the second, third, fourth or fifth segment?

4. In *Castrovalva*, the Portreeve turns out to be which character?

5. Which actor played the Doctor in *The Web of Fear*?

6. What was the name of the pilot show featuring a former robot companion of the Doctor along with human companion, Sarah Jane Smith?

7. Can you unscramble the letters in DISHRAGS to reveal a dangerous creature encountered in *Carnival of Monsters*?

8. In *Snakedance*, what is the name of the planet once ruled by the Mara and then the Manussan Empire?

9. In *Planet of the Daleks*, from what TARDIS item does the Doctor create an anti-Dalek weapon?

10. What was the surname of the Doctor's companion, Tegan?

11. Which planet do Daemons come from: Saturn, Damos, Tridor or Axos?

12. *The Masque of Mandragora* is set during the fifteenth century in which European country?

13. Which is the main city on the planet of Ribos: Shur, Caldos or Skytha?

14. The Rutans were the mortal enemy of which clone-warriors?

15. What is the name of the virus used to defeat the Daleks in *Resurrection of the Daleks*?

16. In *The Mind of Evil*, what missile does the Master hijack: an Alpheus missile, an Alpha-X missile, a Thunderbolt missile or a Terminator missile?

17. Giant Spiders come from which planet?

18. Which *Monty Python* star appeared in a cameo role in *City of Death*?

19. In which story does the first Doctor become invisible whilst Steven Taylor and Dodo Chaplet play a series of strange games?

20. In *The Romans*, who is mistaken by others as Maximus Petullian?

21. In *Battlefield*, what was the name of the character who had the titles, Dominator of the Thirteen Worlds and Battle Queen of Sirax?

22. Which two characters in *Doctor Who: The Movie* does the Doctor bring back from the dead?

23. What was the name of the first story to feature Sylvester McCoy as the Doctor?

24. What is Ace's real first name?

25. In *The Moonbase*, what is the name of the machine based on the Moon that controls the tides on Earth?

26. What was the name of the airline in *The Faceless Ones*?

27. In *The Twin Dilemma*, was the giant gastropod from the planet Jaconda called: Azmael, Mestor, Lexus or Avatar?

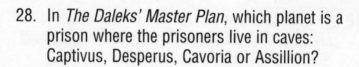

28. In *The Daleks' Master Plan*, which planet is a prison where the prisoners live in caves: Captivus, Desperus, Cavoria or Assillion?

29. In *The Gunfighters*, who hurt their tooth on one of Cyril's sweets, causing them to visit the local dentist, Doc Holliday?

30. In *The Moonbase*, which adversaries of Doctor Who returned to fight him?

31. In *The Green Death*, what was the name of the computer linked to a human brain?

32. In *The Leisure Hive*, Mr Brock and his lawyer turn out to be aliens – but from what reptile-like group?

33. In *The Hand of Fear*, who becomes possessed by a broken stone hand they find in a quarry?

34. Cheetah People and Kitlings appear in which story featuring the seventh Doctor?

35. In the 2004 series of *Doctor Who*, what is the name of Rose's boyfriend?

36. In *The Curse of Fenric*, what is the name of the early computer used to break German codes?

37. In *The Time Warrior*, is Bloodaxe a henchman of: Linx, Sir Edward of Wessex or Irongron?

38. Which story featuring the first Doctor sees the TARDIS arrive in Asia in 1289 and a meeting with Kublai Khan?

39. What happens to a human if they are stung by a Varga plant?

40. What is the name of the replica English village used by the Kraals to prepare for their invasion of Earth?

41. Which companion of the fifth Doctor left him on the prison planet, Sarn?

42. Did the Doctor disguise himself as a gypsy in: *Nightmare of Eden, City of Death* or *The Underwater Menace*?

43. In *The Talons of Weng-Chiang*, what was the name of the killer ventriloquist's dummy: Li-Han, Mr Sin, Weng-Chiang or Gertie?

44. Which robot encountered by the fourth Doctor is made of 'living metal' and has a disintegrator gun?

45. The Psychic Circus is situated on which planet?

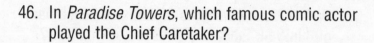

46. In *Paradise Towers*, which famous comic actor played the Chief Caretaker?

47. What was Delia Derbyshire partly responsible for: the *Doctor Who* costumes, the *Doctor Who* title music or the *Doctor Who* scripts?

48. In which story does the Doctor use an emergency system to escape an erupting volcano on Dulkis?

49. In Galaxy 4, whose enemy are the Rills?

50. In *The Talons of Weng-Chiang*, what is the name of the place where Leela and the Doctor attack the dragon?

QUIZ 4

1. What does TARDIS stand for?

2. When Jo Grant reacted to the Master's hypno-sound device, which of the following did she see: a Dalek, a Sea Devil, an Ice Warrior or a Cyberman?

3. In *The Evil of the Daleks*, which two of the following were not a test Dalek: Alpha, Beta, Theta, Omega, Gamma?

4. Who burned down Gabriel Chase house in 1983: the Brigadier, Jo Grant, Ace or Sarah Jane Smith?

5. What tool made its debut in *Fury from the Deep*?

6. In *The Awakening*, who did Will Chandler kill: Tegan, Sir George Hutchinson, Turlough or the Malus?

7. One actor has appeared in episodes of each of the different Doctors: true or false?

8. Actor Pat Gorman has played 15 different roles in the *Doctor Who* episodes over the years: true or false?

9. The second segment of the Key to Time is disguised as which planet: Ribos, Calufrax, Zanak or Dulkis?

10. In *Mission to the Unknown*, which one of the following galaxies was not represented at the Dalek Alliance: Warrien, Celation, Andromeda or Malpha?

11. What is the name of the book which chronicles early Time Lord history: *The Book of the Old Time*, *The Biolog of the Time Lords* or *The Chronicle of Time*?

12. Which episode began the start of *Doctor Who's* twentieth season: *The Arc of Infinity, The Ark in Space* or *The Curse of Peladon*?

13. In *Robot*, the fourth Doctor's pockets contain membership of a table-tennis club from: Venus, Alpha Centauri, Skaro or Inter Minor?

14. The last *Doctor Who* story which featured Tom Baker as the fourth Doctor was called: *Full Circle, The Keeper of Traken, Logopolis* or *Meglos*?

15. Which two companions of the Doctor leave him in a Dalek time machine?

16. In *The Androids of Tara*, who kidnaps Romana: Count Graff, Prince Reynart or Count Grendel?

17. The first *Doctor Who* story which featured Tom Baker as the fourth Doctor was called: *Robot, Logopolis, Full Circle* or *Meglos*?

18. In *The Mind Robber*, after Jamie leaves the TARDIS, what country does he see images of on the scanner?

19. Which of the Doctor's companions was played by actress Katy Manning?

20. What was the name of the dangerous pet kept by Helen A?

21. What is the name of the Beta Dart spaceship in control of the Space Pirates: the White Cross, the Beta Buccaneer or the Delta Destroyer?

22. *The Evil of the Daleks* features which Doctor?

23. Which actor played the Doctor in *Genesis of the Daleks*?

24. What was the name of the *Doctor Who* story which featured Ken Dodd as the Tollmaster?

25. In *The Space Pirates*, who feels spacesick whilst aboard the LIZ 79 spaceship: the Doctor, Jamie or Zoe?

26. In which city is UNIT's headquarters?

27. While the Doctor is in Ashbridge Cottage Hospital, what is his pulse rate measured at?

28. Which actor played the Doctor in *Earthshock*?

29. If you were watching the *Inferno* story, would you see: Professor Stahlman, Professor Zaroff or Professor Brett?

30. In *Genesis of the Daleks*, how long had the Thals and the Kaleds been at war?

31. How frequently do Marshmen emerge from the swamps of their planet?

32. On what planet is *The Space Museum* set?

33. Which one of the following was not a performer at the Psychic Circus in *The Greatest Show in the Galaxy*: Morgana, Flowerchild, Bellboy or Jugglebox?

34. In *The Power of Kroll*, which segment of the Key to Time is swallowed by a giant squid?

35. From which planet was the Doctor given the gift of a time-space visualiser?

36. Which was the third Doctor's most-watched story, according to British viewing figures: *Spearhead from Space, Inferno* or *The Three Doctors*?

37. Which one of the following is not against the law on Terra Alpha: wearing dark clothes, listening to slow music, using an umbrella in the rain?

38. In *The Daemons*, what is the name of the White Witch who helps the Doctor?

39. In which story did Davros first appear:
    The Daleks, Genesis of the Daleks or *Planet of the Daleks*?

40. In *The Time Warrior*, Eleanor, wife of Edward of Wessex, was played by June Brown. She later found fame as which *EastEnders* character?

41. In *Terminus*, who were dependent on the drug hydromel: the Garm, the Vanir or the Sontaran?

42. Who was sent to spy on Vicki but became a companion of the first Doctor?

43. In *The Dalek Invasion of Earth*, is Dalakanium: a metal, an explosive or a medicine?

44. In *Silver Nemesis*, the Nazis and the Cybermen searched for a statue in and around what royal town?

45. In *The Seeds of Death*, who commands the Ice Warriors and are themselves controlled by the Grand Marshal?

46. In *Ghost Light*, which two of the following characters are aliens: Control, Fenn-Cooper, Light, Mrs Grose?

47. In *Warriors of the Deep*, Sentinel Six is: a planet, a satellite, a robot or a computer?

48. In which story did the Imperial Daleks feature?

49. In *Destiny of the Daleks*, who is captured by Tyssan and taken back to Earth to stand trial for his crimes?

50. The Ancient One, Haemovores and Dr Judson all appear in which story featuring the seventh Doctor?

QUIZ 5

1. Which actor replaced Christopher Eccleston as the Doctor?

2. What was the name of the female companion of the Doctor in the first two new series?

3. How many eyes does the Dalek have in the episode, *Dalek*?

4. Do the Ood communicate with humans via a microchip on their forehead, a speaker built into their tongue or a glowing ball they hold?

5. What former ally of the Doctor's is found in the boot of Sarah Jane's car in the episode, *School Reunion*?

6. In *World War Three*, does the RAF, the UN, the CIA or UNIT hold the access codes to the atomic weapons?

7. In *The End of the World*, who is introduced to the other guests as the last living human?

8. What is the name of Rose's mother?

9. Do the Preachers, the Cybermen or John Lumic kidnap Mickey in *Rise of the Cybermen*?

10. In *Love & Monsters*, what is the name of the man who videos his life story and nearly seduces Jackie Tyler?

11. The Game Station on which Rose, Jack and The Doctor are trapped in *Bad Wolf* was formerly: Satellite 5, a Chula spaceship or planet Earth?

12. What sporting event is about to be held in the episode, *Fear Her*?

13. In *Aliens of London*, does the Doctor tell Rose that he is 600, 700, 800 or 900 years old?

14. In what game show does Rose find herself as a contestant in the episode, *Bad Wolf*?

15. In *World War Three*, which famous London house is destroyed to kill the Slitheen?

16. In *The Empty Child*, what colour does the Doctor say is the universal colour for emergency?

17. What name does the Doctor frequently call Mickey Smith to wind him up?

18. In *The Idiot's Lantern*, was the son of the Connolly family called Jackie, Tommy, Chris or Hubert?

19. Is Jefferson, Minister or Bartok head of security in *The Impossible Planet*?

20. In *The Empty Child* what wartime object is fused to the heads of the undead humans all asking for their mummy?

21. What two words does the boy on the bike spray as graffiti on the TARDIS in *Aliens of London*?

22. In *Dalek*, in which US state does the TARDIS arrive at the very start of the episode?

23. In *Rose*, in which city is the transmitter used by the Nestene Consciousness?

24. Whose body does Cassandra flee into after leaving's Rose's in *New Earth*?

25. Is Mr Sneed, Mr Redpath or Mr Dickens the undertaker in *The Unquiet Dead*?

26. What is the name of the alien spirits that the séance in *The Unquiet Dead* makes contact with?

27. In *Aliens of London*, what farmyard animal has been tampered with to appear as an alien in the crashed ship?

28. What is the name of the corporation run by the wheelchair-bound John Lumic in *Rise of the Cybermen*?

29. In *World War Three*, who rescues Jackie from the Slitheen attacking her in her flat?

30. In *Dalek*, who touches the Dalek, setting off a reaction which enables it to break free of its chains in the cage?

31. What is the title of the man who runs Satellite Five's news output and takes his orders from the alien, Jagrafess?

32. In *Father's Day*, when the people are trapped in the church by the aliens, were they there for a wedding, a funeral or a christening?

33. In *Tooth and Claw*, does Flora, Father Angelo or the Doctor threaten Sir Robert's wife to get Sir Robert to commit treason?

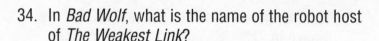

34. In *Bad Wolf*, what is the name of the robot host of *The Weakest Link*?

35. In *The Idiot's Lantern*, where is the London location of the giant television transmitter that Magpie and the Doctor climb?

36. In *The Satan's Pit*, who failed to make it past junction 8.1 and died due to loss of air?

37. Which comedienne and actress appears in a bridal gown in the TARDIS at the very end of the second series?

38. In *School Reunion*, is the name of the theory that controls the parts that make up the Universe: the Krillitane Paradox, the Scasis Paradigm or the Unifying Field?

39. Which man kisses Rose and then the Doctor in *The Parting of the Ways*?

40. Which creatures insist on serving humans as they have nothing else in their lives, in *The Impossible Planet*?

41. In the episode, *Rose*, what type of car, coloured yellow, does Mickey drive Rose in?

42. The episode *Tooth and Claw* is set in which country in 1879?

43. Are the Sisters of Plenitude in *New Earth* breeding Cybermen, humans, Sycorax or bacteria to inflict illnesses on?

44. In *The Christmas Invasion*, which part of the Doctor's body did the Sycorax cut off?

45. Which two people are with the Doctor in *The Idiot's Lantern* when he breaks into Magpie's television shop?

46. What type of medal does Rose say she got in gymnastics shortly before swinging on a chain to knock one of the mannequins into the Nestene Consciousness to save the Doctor?

47. In *Doomsday*, Dr Rajesh Singh is the first character that what item of the Doctor's doesn't work on?

48. In *Love & Monsters*, what is the name of the Chinese restaurant Elton tells Ursula he is taking her to?

49. The name of what planet (also a European city) is the last word the Doctor says at the end of the first series straight after he has regenerated?

50. In *Bad Wolf*, how many credits is Rodrick told he has gained for winning *The Weakest Link*?

1. In *The Sun Makers*, the reward offered for the Doctor's capture is how many Talmars: 50, 500, 5,000, 500,000 or five million?

2. In *The Green Death*, who nurses Professor Jones back to life after he is bitten by a Giant Maggot?

3. In *Four to Doomsday*, the Urbankans are like giant versions of what Earth creatures?

4. Which actor played the Doctor in *The Caves of Androzani*?

5. In *Death to the Daleks*, after the TARDIS loses all power at the start of the story, what planet does it materialise on?

6. Which Professor encountered in *The Underwater Menace* has a pet octopus?

7. In *Remembrance of the Daleks*, what is the name of the Dalek containing Davros?

8. In *The War Machines*, which Professor is taken over by his own creation?

9. In *Kinda*, when the Mara appeared as a giant snake, the Doctor finally trapped it inside a circle of what?

10. In *Revelation of the Daleks*, what part of Orcini's body is artificial?

11. In *Terror of the Zygons*, what is the name of the Scottish village where UNIT set up a temporary base: Connagh, Tullock, Aviness or Dunvale?

12. Which *Doctor Who* adversary's key weakness is the probic vent situated in the back of their neck?

13. The son of Hollywood star Errol Flynn appeared in *The Wheel in Space* as Leo Ryan: true or false?

14. In *Resurrection of the Daleks*, who do the Daleks seek to break out of prison to help them find an antidote to a virus?

15. In *The Tenth Planet*, what creatures came with the arrival of a new planet in the solar system?

16. In *Resurrection of the Daleks*, which of the Doctor's companions is injured by a Dalek attack?

17. In which *Doctor Who* story was one of the Doctor's companions given the alias Miss Dodo Dupont?

18. In *Doctor Who and the Silurians*, the actor who played Avon in *Blake's 7* played UNIT's Captain Hawkins. What is the actor's name?

19. In *The Evil of the Daleks*, what is the name of the antiques dealer who stole the TARDIS?

20. Which creatures were made extinct when a space freighter exploded on Earth millions of years ago?

21. Which creatures are eight feet tall and invisible: the Sea Devils, the Mechanoids or the Visians?

22. In *Silver Nemesis*, the Doctor plays a jazz tape on Ace's ghettoblaster to blast communications signals from what adversaries?

23. MSC stands for: Marine Space Corps, Martian Shock Catapult or Matter Serial Compressor?

24. In *The Two Doctors*, who had fitted a Stattenheim remote control to the second Doctor's TARDIS?

25. Which War Machine was the Doctor able to reprogram to destroy WOTAN: War Machine Number 7, War Machine Number 9 or War Machine Number 13?

26. Who did Jo Grant fall in love with and give up travelling with the Doctor for?

27. What is the name of the Daleks' foe on the planet Mechanus?

28. Barbara Wright and Ian Chesterton finally returned to Earth in an old time capsule previously owned by which *Doctor Who* adversaries?

29. Andrew Verney was whose grandfather: Tegan's, Jo's, Nyssa's or Romana's?

30. In *Death to the Daleks*, the Doctor and Sarah prepare to take a holiday in: Flours 7, Florida or Florana?

31. In *The Krotons*, which companion does the Doctor tell he is not a doctor of medicine?

32. Which story was shown first: *The Happiness Patrol, The Leisure Hive* or *The Macra Terror*?

33. Which *Doctor Who* character used a weapon called the Tissue Compression Eliminator?

34. In *The Visitation*, which airport does the Doctor take Tegan Jovanka to, only to arrive 200 years too early?

35. Which actor who played the Doctor had previously appeared in the show as Commander Maxil?

36. In *The Sea Devils*, which 1970s children's television show does the Master watch in his cell?

37. In *Death to the Daleks*, the Doctor recognises that he has seen Exxilon symbols before on Earth – but in which South American country?

38. The star of *The Chinese Detective* TV show, David Yip, appeared in which Daleks-based story?

39. What does the Master's hypnotic-sound device make creatures see?

40. In *Spearhead from Space*, which military force shoots the Doctor?

41. Which Doctor dressed up as Sherlock Holmes in a story: the fourth Doctor, the fifth Doctor or the sixth Doctor?

42. In *City of Death*, how many copies of the Mona Lisa is Leonardo da Vinci persuaded to paint in addition to the original?

43. In *The Gunfighters*, which ally of the Clanton Brothers was killed in a shootout?

44. In *Delta and the Bannermen*, an American satellite knocks a space bus off-course to land in 1959 in which country?

45. In *The Deadly Assassin*, what is the name of the Chancellor who dies after a struggle with the Doctor?

46. Boscowan Moor is the home of: UNIT's secret headquarters, Davros's hideout on Earth or the Nine Travellers group of standing stones?

47. In *The Web Planet*, the Animus control which creature: the Voord, the Zarbi or the Menoptra?

48. In *The Keeper of Traken*, who marries Tremas?

49. In the first series of the show, at what school did Barbara Wright teach when she encountered the Doctor?

50. In *The Keys of Marinus*, Arbitan is the keeper of what entity?

1. In *The Underwater Menace*, what legendary place is destroyed in the future by a scientist's experiments?

2. And what was the name of the scientist?

3. Which story featured a newly-regenerated Romana?

4. In *Arc of Infinity*, which of his former adversaries does the Doctor kill: Omega, Davros or the Wirrn?

5. Which *Doctor Who* story was set in Amsterdam and filmed on location in the Netherlands?

6. In *The Ambassadors of Death*, astronauts are kidnapped and replaced by aliens while they are returning from a mission to which planet?

7. Which story saw the debut of Dr Liz Smith as a companion?

8. Jon Pertwee played both Meglos and the Doctor in the story *Meglos*: true or false?

9. In *State of Decay*, what was the former identity of Aukon?

10. In *The Leisure Hive*, what item was used to strangle Stimson to death?

11. What story was the last to feature Jo Grant as the Doctor's companion?

12. In which story, set around oil exploration, does the second Doctor fly a helicopter?

13. The end of *The Caves of Androzani* marks the arrival of which actor as Doctor Who?

14. In *Pyramids of Mars*, is the name of the Osiran who destroyed his own planet: Scarman, Horus, Sutekh or Amhotep?

15. In *Marco Polo*, what was the name of the warlord looking to assassinate Kublai Khan?

16. Who does Azal the Daemon offer its powers to: the Master, the Doctor or the Daleks?

17. Which actor who played Doctor Who died in 1996?

18. The last episode featuring the seventh Doctor was shown on the BBC in December of which year?

19. In *The Dominators*, which *Play School* and *Play Away* star played the role of Tensa?

20. Which enemy of the Doctor's is shrunk to a very small size as he looks for numismaton gas on the planet Sarn?

21. In *Vengeance on Varos*, which two of the following three characters were rebels: Jondar, Quillam, Areta?

22. In *Mawdryn Undead*, Tegan and which other companion are regressed to children?

23. On which planet would you find a Raston Warrior Robot?

24. With whom does Doctor Who make a form of pact to fight the warriors of Exxilon?

25. On Earth, Scaroth disguises himself as: Count Scarlioni, William Shakespeare, the Brigadier or Eric Klieg?

26. In which country were the Giant Maggots created?

27. Can you name either the comedy actor or actress who played eccentric art dealers in *City of Death*?

28. Which type of warhead kills any creature with a central nervous system: a Konton warhead, a Bendalypse warhead or a Votar warhead?

29. In *The Daleks*, who leaves a batch of anti-radiation pills outside the TARDIS?

30. What are the name of the stone-like creatures from the planet Orgros who feed on blood?

31. What were the name of the two companions who witnessed the first regeneration of Doctor Who?

32. Which of the second Doctor's stories received the highest viewing figures in Britain: *The Moonbase, The War Games* or *The Mind Robber*?

33. In *Ghost Light*, what is the name of the Neanderthal man who was Josiah Smith's butler?

34. In *The Mark of the Rani*, whose TARDIS is disguised as a cupboard: the Master's, the Doctor's or the Rani's?

35. Who is the last of the Daemons: Azal, Bessie, Ogron or Magister?

36. In *Paradise Towers*, what surprising feature of the TARDIS is said to be jettisoned: the cricket pavilion, the swimming pool or the car park?

37. In which *Doctor Who* story does the Monk's TARDIS turn into a Saxon sarcophagus?

38. The grandson of an actor who played Doctor Who played cricket for England in 2003. Who was he?

39. What colour was the antique car that the third Doctor stole to escape from hospital in his first story?

40. In *The Two Doctors*, which Doctor was found by the sixth Doctor to be captured and held by the Sontarans?

41. In *Frontios*, what does a meteorite bombardment appear to destroy?

42. At the start of *The Underwater Menace*, how many characters inside the TARDIS are seen thinking about where they would like to land next?

43. In *The Mutants*, who sends the Doctor and Jo to deliver a message canister to the planet Solos?

44. Which of the two alien creatures in *Ghost Light* assumed a female form?

45. In *The King's Demons*, Sir Giles Estram's surname is an anagram of which *Doctor Who* character?

46. Which frequent enemy of the Doctor has a degree in Cosmic Science?

47. In *The Mind Robber*, what is the name of the land populated by characters including Gulliver and Rapunzel?

48. The son of an actor who played James Bond played Jondar in *Vengeance on Varos*. Who was he?

49. Which one of the following *Doctor Who* stories is notable because no characters die: *The Seeds of Doom*, *The War Games*, *Snakedance*, *Vengeance on Varos*?

50. At the end of *The War Games* story, to which planet is the Doctor exiled by the Time Lords?

QUIZ 8

1. The first Doctor visited a city which stood on 1,500 foot-high stilts and giant mushroom-like plants, which could move. Which planet was this on?

2. In *The Ark in Space*, what child's toy does the Doctor use to take a gravity reading?

3. Which one of the following stories did not feature the TARDIS: *The Invisible Enemy*, *Genesis of the Daleks* or *Nightmare of Eden*?

4. In *The Tomb of the Cybermen*, the Doctor says he is approximately: 250, 450, 1,500 or 10,500 years old?

5. In *The Tenth Planet*, whose son is in a second space capsule sent up to help a first space capsule?

6. In *Horror of Fang Rock*, what were the name of the evil, shape-changing creatures which evolved on the planet Ruta 3?

7. Jean Marsh played which *Doctor Who* character: Ace, Sara Kingdom, Zoe Heriot or Leela?

8. What is the name of the Paradise Towers resident who lures the architect Kroagnon into a trap, but dies as a result?

9. In *The Moonbase*, which one of the following is not a geologist: Ralph, Nils, Franz or Jules?

10. What was the name of the creator of the K-1 robot?

11. The son of an actor who played Doctor Who appeared as Private Moor in *The War Games*. Can you name him?

12. What relation does Susan Foreman say she is to the Doctor?

13. Dr Grace Holloway was one of the fourth Doctor's companions: true or false?

14. In which story does the Doctor visit Tibet to return a sacred bell to a monastery?

15. Which two of the following were members of The Brotherhood of Logicians: Eric Klieg, Professor Clifford Jones, Prince Reynart, Kaftan?

16. Can you name either of the twins kidnapped by Professor Edgeworth in *The Twin Dilemma*?

17. In *The Caves of Androzani*, who spills some of the antidote to Spectrox Toxaemia?

18. The Solonians mutate into huge versions of what type of creature: insects, apes, fish or vultures?

19. The Destroyer can be killed by bullets made from which metal?

20. Which three of the fourth Doctor's companions are present when he regenerates into the fifth Doctor?

21. In the first *Doctor Who* story, the firemaker and the leader of the tribe was the father of: Horg, Za or Kal?

22. Which tool of the Doctor's was destroyed during *The Visitation*?

23. In *The Curse of Peladon*, delegate Alpha Centauri had just one large eye – but how many arms?

24. In *City of Death*, which famous Earth painting does Scaroth plan to steal?

25. What is the title of the figure in charge of the sixth Doctor's trial?

26. In *The Three Doctors*, which of the Doctors is caught in a time eddy and can only observe and advise?

27. Which actor played the Doctor in *The Daleks' Master Plan*?

28. In *Dragonfire*, what is the freezing-cold name of the space trading outpost on the planet Svartos?

29. Which actor who played Doctor Who broke his collar bone and had to use a double for scenes during the filming of *The Sontaran Experiment*?

30. In *The Underwater Menace*, what is the name of the mad scientist trying to raise Atlantis?

31. On what planet would you find Arbitan and the Conscience Machine?

32. What nationality was the Doctor's companion, Tegan?

33. Who emerge from seed pods to infect humans or animals: the Krynoid, Marshmen or Zygons?

34. Dr Judson created a code-breaking machine in *The Curse of Fenric*, which was set during which war?

35. In *The Faceless Ones*, what is the name of the creatures who wish to kidnap 50,000 young humans and replace them on Earth?

36. In *The Deadly Assassin*, viewers learn that a Time Lord can undergo how many regenerations?

37. Who is the youngest Argolin on Argolis who plans to create a warlike army of clones?

38. Which *Doctor Who* companion graduated from the Time Lord Academy with a triple First and is almost 140 years of age when she first meets the Doctor?

39. Which Doctor strips off and wears just a shower cap to take a shower, as part of his escape from Ashbridge Cottage Hospital?

40. In *Logopolis*, what telescope's walkway did the fourth Doctor fall off of?

41. In *Invasion of the Dinosaurs*, what type of dinosaur does the Brigadier keep at bay in a London tube station, using a cigarette lighter?

42. What colour was the body of the Imperial Daleks?

43. Doctor Who transports Marcus Scarman to which planet?

44. In *The Chase*, what sphere-shaped creature has flamethrowers as weapons?

45. Which alien turns Gwendoline Pritchard and her mother into stone so that they will never change again?

46. In *Revelation of the Daleks*, the Doctor travels to Tranquil Repose to visit the body of which friend?

47. In *The Moonbase*, the hurricane which struck Florida was named: Lucy, Oscar, Harold or Benjamin?

48. In *State of Decay*, were The Three Who Rule: vampires, Silurians, Sea Devils or Ice Warriors?

49. In *City of Death*, Scaroth is living on Earth in the year: 1849, 1929, 1979 or 2019?

50. The company Ratcliffe's Builders' Merchants featured in which *Doctor Who* story?

QUIZ 9

1. In *The Dominators*, what is the name of the island on Dulkis which was used for atomic testing?

2. What was the name of the first story to feature Patrick Troughton as the Doctor?

3. In *Spearhead from Space*, what is the name of the poacher who hides a meteorite from space but eventually tells UNIT?

4. In *State of Decay*, can you name two out of the three members of the spacecraft, Hydrax, who became The Three Who Rule?

5. In *The Time Monster*, which member of UNIT is regressed into a baby?

6. What does UNIT stand for?

7. *Time-Flight* sees the TARDIS arrive at Heathrow airport to investigate an aircraft which has gone missing. What type of aircraft is this?

8. In *Remembrance of the Daleks*, what is the name of the leader of the Rebel Daleks?

9. Which character has been played at different times by the following actors: Roger Delgado, Peter Pratt and Geoffrey Beevers?

10. In *The Tenth Planet*, does ISC stand for: Intarus Space Colony, Interruptible Space Continuum or International Space Command?

11. What three-letter name is given to an indestructible gargoyle brought to life by the Daemons?

12. What type of bomb does General Cutler try to launch at the Cybermen's planet?

13. In *Mission to the Unknown*, which flags were found on the tail fins of Marc Cory's spaceship: Union Jack flags, Stars and Stripes flags or French flags?

14. By what shortened name was Dorothea Chaplet better known?

15. In *Robot*, what is the name of the organisation trying to blackmail the world's governments: the Black Watch, the Scientific Reform Society or the Space Watch Alliance?

16. Which Doctor was the first to use a sonic screwdriver?

17. In *Revenge of the Cybermen*, what is the name of the legendary planet of gold: Nerva, Augmor or Voga?

18. Which two of these disguises did Doctor Who adopt in *The Highlanders*: a British soldier, a farmer, a washerwoman, a priest?

19. Which enemies of the Doctor firebomb London using boxes which feature three dials on their fronts?

20. Which was the first *Doctor Who* story to be broadcast in the 1970s?

21. Whose TARDIS key did Ben and Polly return to the Doctor: Dodo Chaplet's or Steven Taylor's?

22. Which actor played the Doctor in *Inferno*?

23. In *Meglos*, the mercenaries led by General Grugger are called: Deons, Tigellans or Gaztaks?

24. What is the name of the millionaire plant collector who ties up his assistant, Keeler, and becomes possessed by the Krynoid?

25. In *The Awakening*, the people of Little Hodcombe plan to re-enact which famous English war?

26. According to the book, *Doctor Who: The Legend*, which *Doctor Who* story polled the highest ever viewer ratings in Britain?

27. In *Revenge of the Cybermen*, which creation of the Cybermen does the Doctor use to attack them?

28. In *The Talons of Weng-Chiang*, who does Leela call 'bent face': Magnus Greel, Henry Jago or Professor Litefoot?

29. What was the name of the second story to feature the Autons?

30. Which planet-sucking creature could be killed by salt?

31. Name the two *Doctor Who* actors who in real life trained as monks?

32. In *Spearhead from Space*, did the Doctor discover the real Major General Scobie in: Windsor Castle, Madame Tussaud's, Tower Bridge or Heathrow airport?

33. In *The Brain of Morbius*, what is the name of the group who guard the Elixir of Life and bring down any spaceship which travels near to their planet, Karn?

34. What was the name of the Brigadier's wife?

35. Which famous horror film actor played the Black Guardian in four *Doctor Who* stories?

36. In *The Dominators*, what tool of the Doctor's converts into a blowtorch to cut through a wall?

37. In *Remembrance of the Daleks*, were the Daleks on Earth in: 1843, 1963, 1993 or 2043?

38. Which one of the following *Doctor Who* stories features no loss of life: *Remembrance of the Daleks, The Mind Robber, Planet of Evil* or *Nightmare of Eden*?

39. Which adversaries of Doctor Who are powered by static electricity?

40. In *The War Games*, what was the name of the time-travel machines which used technology similar to the TARDIS?

41. In *The Happiness Patrol*, who is the Kandyman's assistant: Helen A, Gilbert M or Joseph C?

42. Who murdered Victoria Waterfield's father, making her an orphan?

43. In *The Caves of Androzani*, what vegetable does the doctor carry to warn him of deadly gases?

44. And what colour does the vegetable turn if the deadly gases are present?

45. The actor behind which *Coronation Street* character played the part of Malpha in *Doctor Who*: Alf Roberts, Stan Ogden or Mike Baldwin?

46. In *Spearhead from Space*, what is the name of the senior military officer who liaised with UNIT and is replaced by a plastic replica?

47. What is the name of the business partner of Hardon's who is found dead on Argolis, hanged by the Doctor's scarf?

48. In which story is the Doctor both court-martialled during an Earth war and put on trial by the Time Lords?

49. Which actor played the Doctor in *The Tomb of the Cybermen*?

50. What is the name of the Cybermen's world, revealed in *The Tenth Planet*?

QUIZ 10

1. In *Destiny of the Daleks*, who does Princess Romana regenerate into?

2. In which *Doctor Who* story do the Daleks frighten the crew and passengers of the Marie Celeste?

3. In *Underworld*, is the tunnel system known as: the tree, the labyrinth or the network?

4. The Brotherhood of Logicians is: a cover name for UNIT, a secret society or another name for a gathering of Time Lords?

5. Which *Doctor Who* actor had roles in the films *Phantom of the Opera*, *The Omen* and *Jason and the Argonauts*?

6. In *The Two Doctors*, what is the name of the Androgum which Dastari wants to turn into a god?

7. What was the name of the ITV show which Jon Pertwee hosted immediately after leaving *Doctor Who*?

8. In *Fury from the Deep*, what medical instrument does the Doctor use to listen to sounds in the pipeline on the beach?

9. What symbol can be found on the collar of the fifth Doctor's shirt?

10. In *The Green Death*, the director of which company had his brain linked to a computer?

11. In *Inferno*, the Brigade Leader in the alternate world has an eyepatch over which eye?

12. In *The Ark*, what planet is the ark spacecraft travelling to?

13. In *Revenge of the Cybermen*, what is the planet of gold also known as: Voga, Trion, Skaros or Aurium?

14. In *Attack of the Cybermen*, the Cybermen establish a base in the sewers of which city?

15. In *State of Decay*, how many arrow-class scout ships can detach from the Hydrax ship?

16. In *The Armageddon Factor*, which two of the following planets are at war with each other: Delta Magna, Atrios, Vovos, Zeos?

17. Do Swampies call humans: Longhairs, Two-Eyes or Dryfoots?

18. What was the name of the man nicknamed the Butcher of Brisbane?

19. Whose Trilogic game does the Doctor destroy from inside his TARDIS?

20. Which story, featuring the first Doctor, takes place entirely inside the TARDIS?

21. Who pays Orcini to assassinate Davros: Kara, Peri, the sixth Doctor or the Master?

22. In *The Underwater Menace*, is the ruler of Atlantis called: Aqua, Ravellin, Thous or Gentos?

23. In *The Armageddon Factor*, what is the name of the sixth princess of the sixth dynasty of the sixth royal house of Atrios?

24. In *The Myth Makers*, who appears out of the TARDIS, stopping the Trojans from burning it: Vicki, Steven Taylor or Katarina?

25. In which story does the Doctor and his companions encounter an expedition at Telos, financed by Kaftan, and seeking to revive the Cybermen?

26. What does the Doctor diagnose is poisoning and killing the Sensorites: cyanide, arsenic, belladonna or radiation?

27. The Nestenes brought to life plastic mannequins known by what name?

28. Which alien race created an android replica of Harry Sullivan: the Krotons, the Kralls or the Autons?

29. The Doomsday Weapon is said to be designed to explode what object in space?

30. When Brigadier Lethbridge-Stewart first featured on the *Doctor Who* show, what rank did he hold?

31. Which two of the following did not have their own TARDIS: the Master, Professor Brett, Auxon, Omega?

32. In *The Krotons*, what does HADS stand for?

33. In *The Savages*, what is the name of the scientist who channels life forces to feed the Council of Elders?

34. When the sixth Doctor regenerates into the seventh Doctor, which character is attacking the TARDIS?

35. What is the name of the planet which two conmen try to sell Vynda-K: Ribos, Skaro, Inter Minor or Selestrian?

36. Which Kastrian designed his regenerated body in the shape of one of the Doctor's companions?

37. And which *Doctor Who* companion was it?

38. The Zygons lived in which British lake?

39. International Space Control runs the Moonbase in the story of the same name – but in which European city is its headquarters?

40. Which Doctor collapses on the floor of the TARDIS's control room and is watched by Ben and Polly as he regenerates?

41. In *The Celestial Toymaker*, the Toymaker has a lifespan of 300 years: true or false?

42. The fifth Doctor claims he once took five wickets for which Australian state cricket team?

43. Which of the first Doctor's stories received the highest British viewing figures: *The Smugglers*, *The Celestial Toymaker* or *The Web Planet*?

44. Which is the first of the Doctor's companions to be killed in the show?

45. Which one of the following stories did not feature the TARDIS: *The Sea Devils, The Space Pirates* or *The Krotons*?

46. In *The Ark*, where is the spaceship carrying samples of Earth life heading to: Trion, Refusis II or Argolis?

47. The actor who played Vila in *Blake's 7* featured as Goudry in which fourth Doctor story?

48. Leonard de Vries is killed by a standing stone in which story featuring the fourth Doctor?

49. Which giant insect-like creatures were first spotted by humans in the Andromeda galaxy?

50. What is the name of the creator of the statue in *Silver Nemesis*: Davros, Lady Peinforte, Rassilon or Sutekh?

QUIZ 11

1. Did Christopher Eccleston or David Tennant star as the Doctor in *The Satan Pit*?

2. What is Elton Pope's favourite band in *Love & Monsters*: The Who, The Space Cowboys or the Electric Light Orchestra?

3. The very first episode of the new series was named after which character?

4. Which former British monarch do the Doctor and Rose meet in *Tooth and Claw*?

5. In *The Impossible Planet*, is the nickname of the planet by the black hole, 'the siren', 'the dark star' or 'the bitter pill'?

6. At the end of *Bad Wolf*, which former enemies of the Doctor hold Rose captive?

7. In *The Age of Steel*, which character vows to stay behind in the parallel universe to ours to help make up for the loss of Ricky?

8. In *The Christmas Invasion*, what is the name of the new female Prime Minister of Britain?

9. Does Rose pose as an A-Level student, a student teacher or a dinner lady in the episode, *School Reunion*?

10. What does the Empty Child in the episode of the same name keep on asking for?

11. In *The Idiot's Lantern*, does the Doctor capture the Wire in a single television, inside his sonic screwdriver or in a Betamax video cassette?

12. Is Suki, Cathica or Trilla the name of the female journalist who gets promoted to Floor 500 at the start of the episode, *The Long Game*?

13. What is the last image that Chloe draws before the Isolus leaves her, in *Fear Her*?

14. In *The Doctor Dances*, who teleports just himself out of trouble, leaving the Doctor and Rose?

15. In *The Satan's Pit*, how many miles down from the space station is the planet: 10, 100, 1,000 or 10,000 miles?

16. The ghosts in *Army of Ghosts* turn into which former enemy of the Doctor?

17. In *Love & Monsters*, what is the name of the planet that the alien played by Peter Kay comes from?

18. What item of Rose's does Mickey bring her near the start of the episode, *Boom Town*?

19. In *Father's Day*, does Jackie Tyler tell Rose that her Dad died in a plane crash, a terrorist explosion or a hit and run accident?

20. Which former companion of the Doctor's appears as a journalist in the episode, *School Reunion*?

21. In *World War Three*, in which sea does the Doctor say that the Slitheen have a spaceship?

22. Major Blake and Danny Llewellyn are killed by which alien life forms: the Sycorax, the Cybermen or the Nestene Consciousness?

23. Does a monster made of lead, steel, graphite or diamond attack Rose when she opens a garage in *Fear Her*?

24. On Captain Jack Harkness's ship, Emergency Protocol 417 results in: firing an escape pod, putting the crew into suspended animation or making a cocktail?

25. Who tries to teach the Doctor to dance in the episode, *The Doctor Dances*?

26. In which episode of the first new series was Rose disintegrated when she lost in a game show?

27. In *The Parting of the Ways*, which planet does the lead Dalek order to be purified with fire?

28. Mickey finds a huge collection of what vacuum-packed creature in *School Reunion*?

29. In *New Earth*, is the name of the giant city New London, New Paris or New New York?

30. In *Aliens of London*, who do Rose and Harriet find dead in a cupboard in 10 Downing Street?

31. What old adversary of the Doctor's is the last remaining member of its kind chained in an underground bunker by Henry van Statten?

32. In *The Long Game*, does a head chip inserted into the back of the skull cost 100, 1,000 or 10,000 credits on Satellite 5?

33. Using a zip on what part of the body do the Slitheen remove their human disguise to show their alien form?

34. Whose computer does Rose use in the first episode of the first new series to try and find out about the Doctor?

35. Who accidentally opens the Genesis Ark by touching it in *Doomsday*: the Doctor, Rose, Jackie Tyler or Mickey?

36. Does Bridget, Mr Skinner, Victor Kennedy or Ursula Blake turn out to be an alien in *Love & Monsters*?

37. Which member of the space station in *The Impossible Planet* is an archeologist who finds himself suddenly covered in ancient writing?

38. Does the Doctor reveal to Rose that he is a Time Lord in *Boom Town*, *Rose*, *The End of the World* or *Aliens of London*?

39. In *The Empty Child*, to which hospital does Nancy take the Doctor in order to meet Doctor Constantine?

40. What is the name of the female *Big Brother* contestant who befriends the Doctor in *Bad Wolf*?

41. In *Doomsday*, the Doctor opens the breach to stop the Daleks and Cybermen at the top of which building?

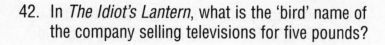

42. In *The Idiot's Lantern*, what is the 'bird' name of the company selling televisions for five pounds?

43. In *The Christmas Invasion*, the Sycorax take over all the people on Earth with what type blood group?

44. In *Army of Ghosts*, which member of Rose's family does Jackie Tyler says is coming to visit shortly even though he died years ago?

45. In *The End of the World*, which guest's gift to Rose and the Doctor is to spit in Rose's face?

46. In *Boom Town*, what is the name of the nuclear power station being built in a Welsh city?

47. *The Unquiet Dead* sees Rose and the Doctor arrive in which British town in 1869?

48. What was the name of the actress whose character replaced Billie Piper's as the Doctor's companion for the third series?

49. In *Rose*, what is the house number on the wheelie bin that consumes Mickey Smith while Rose is talking to Clive?

50. Whose Greatest Hits poster does Rose spot at the start of the episode, *Fear Her*, indicating that she and the Doctor are in the near future?

1. What is the name of the holiday camp in which much of *Delta and the Bannermen* is set?

2. Who does the Doctor hypnotise in *The Abominable Snowmen*?

3. *Fury from the Deep* is set along the coast of which sea?

4. What planet is the only known source of Zeiton 7, needed by the sixth Doctor to repair the Tardis?

5. What is the name of the lake which lies close to Dalek City, which contains water that glows in the dark?

6. In *The Leisure Hive*, a tachyon surge ages the Doctor by: 100 years, 300 years or 500 years?

7. In *Terror of the Zygons*, what is the name of the dinosaur-like creature used by the Zygons and housed in Loch Ness?

8. In *Carnival of Monsters*, was the name of the ship the Doctor and Jo landed on: the *Marie Celeste*, the *SS Bernice*, *HMS Braveheart* or the *Atlantis Traveller*?

9. In *Trial of a Time Lord*, who handles the defence for the sixth Doctor?

10. In *The Web of Fear*, the robot Yeti infest what transport system?

11. What is the name of the computer worshipped by the Sevateem as a God: WOTAN, Xoanon or BOSS?

12. In *The Brain of Morbius*, whose head does Solon want to use to reconstruct Morbius?

13. By what shortened name was Perpugilliam Brown better known, whilst she was a companion of the Doctor?

14. What is officially called Station Three: the Silver Carrier, the Moonbase or the Wheel?

15. What job does Shockeye perform on the space station: pilot, chef, philosopher, mechanic or weapons controller?

16. In *The Smugglers*, was the name of Avery's ship: the Dark Cloud, the Black Albatross or the Saucy Gull?

17. Steven Taylor was one of the Doctor's companions. Can you name the actor who played him?

18. On whose orders does K-9 enter the sea at Brighton to fetch a beachball, only to suffer a major short-circuit?

19. Did Doctor Who disguise himself as a mummy in: *The Pyramids of Mars, The Sun Makers* or *The Aztecs*?

20. In the very first TV episode, how far into the past did Doctor Who and his companions journey to help cavemen?

21. In *The Myth Makers* is the Doctor captured by: Greeks, Egyptians, Trojans or Romans?

22. In *The Dalek Invasion of Earth*, what is the name of the humans turned into living robots by the Daleks?

23. Which of the following Aztecs was the High Priest of Knowledge: Autloc, Tlotoxl or Cameca?

24. In which story did plastic mannequins all over Britain break out of their shop windows and kill people?

25. In *The Ambassadors of Death*, General Carrington is the head of what department?

26. In *The Dominators*, what was the name given to the robots used by the Dominators?

27. Toxic waste poured into a disused mine created which of Doctor Who's adversaries: Cybermen, the Wirrn, Giant Maggots or the Nimon?

28. Who released the monster, Kronos, which destroys Atlantis?

29. Jamie Mackimmon joined the Doctor as a companion in which story?

30. In the Travelmat Relay system, which one of these is not a city on its Moonbase control board: Washington, Izmir, Sydney, London?

31. In *The Leisure Hive*, what sport is demonstrated by Pangol being played in the Recreation Generator?

32. In *The Mark of the Rani*, what was the name of the lord who had invited many celebrated Victorian engineers for a gathering?

33. Which enemies of the Doctor's plan to fire a plague missile at Exxilon but are thwarted when Galloway, an ally of the third Doctor, explodes a bomb on their ship?

34. What game consists of a pyramid of layers and must be completed in 1,023 moves?

35. What colour do the Happiness Patrol paint the Doctor's TARDIS?

36. Which old Gallifrey colleague of the Doctor's was sentenced to 10 years in Brixton jail and built the computer, Mentalis?

37. What was the name of the Madame Chairman of Argolis: Mena, Morix, Miyuna or Maria?

38. What was the first story to feature Peter Davison as the Doctor?

39. In *Doctor Who: The Movie*, a member of a San Franciscan street gang accompanies the injured Doctor to hospital. Who is this?

40. The spiders in *Planet of the Spiders* are led by: Queen Huath, Abbott Kianpo, Abbot Cho-Je or King Peladon?

41. In *The Krotons*, how many suns orbit the planet where the Gonds live?

42. Which BBC newsreader appeared as himself in *The War Machines*?

43. Which adversaries of the Doctor made their debut in *The Tenth Planet*?

44. Yartek was the leader of: the Sontarans, the Ice Warriors or the Voord?

45. *Terror of the Autons* saw the arrival of which of Doctor Who's companions: Sarah Jane Smith, Jo Grant, Zoe Heriot or Susan Foreman?

46. In *The Happiness Patrol*, what colour was the Kandyman's head?

47. Which rainforest region did Clifford Jones and Jo Grant head off to explore?

48. Which of the Doctor's companions accidentally kills Vicki's pet Sand Beast?

49. The sixth Doctor contracts the deadly disease, Spectrox Toxaemia, on which planet?

50. In *The Space Museum*, the Doctor disguised himself as an exhibit of which of his enemies?

QUIZ 13

1. In *The Daleks' Master Plan*, what terrifying weapon do the Daleks plan to deploy?

2. In *The Time Meddler*, who did the Monk meet to discuss powered flight: the Wright Brothers, Leonardo da Vinci or the Montgolfier brothers?

3. *The Reign of Terror* was set during the time of which military leader: Ghengis Khan, Napoleon or Alexander the Great?

4. In *Black Orchid*, the relic in the attic turns out to be which of Charles Cranleigh's relations: his brother, his wife or his grandmother?

5. Which of the Doctor's female companions had a degree in pure mathematics?

6. In *The Space Pirates*, are the beacons powered by: solar energy, static electricity or uranium isotopes?

7. In *Doctor Who: The Movie*, what is the name of the cardiologist who is taken over by the Master?

8. What is the name of the guardian of the solar system who the Doctor meets in *The Daleks' Master Plan*?

9. In which *Doctor Who* story is the Doctor mistaken for the great lyre player, Pettulian?

10. In *Arc of Infinity*, who was the traitor who betrays the Doctor: Borusa, Councillor Hedin or Azmael?

11. Which airforce destroy the Krynoid plant just before it can eject thousands of dangerous seed pods?

12. Helen A was the leader of which planet: Skaro, Sigma 7 or Terra Alpha?

13. In *Full Circle*, the TARDIS lands on Alzarius when the fourth Doctor is heading to which planet?

14. Do the Dominators in the story of the same name have: one heart, two hearts or no heart?

15. In *The Gunfighters*, which of the Doctor's companions uses the alias Steven Regret?

16. In *The War Machines*, which professor was taken over by his creation, WOTAN?

17. In *The Seeds of Death*, what colour are the Martian seed pods?

18. Terry Nation is credited with devising the Daleks. He also wrote jokes for which popular 1960s comedian?

19. After Vicki's mother died, her father took a job on: Skaro, Astra or Venus?

20. In *The Underwater Menace*, what is the name of the creatures fitted with plastic gills so that they can breathe and work underwater?

21. In *The Wheel in Space*, what is the name of the Controller of the Wheel: Zoe Heriot, Jarvis Bennett, John Robson or Maggie Harris?

22. What colour skins do the Axons have at the start of *The Claws of Axos*?

23. Which one of the following was not a TV story of *Doctor Who: The War Games, The War Machines* or *Arrangements for War*?

24. In *Arc of Infinity*, which of the Doctor's companions was captured by the Ergon?

25. Which story was shown first: *The Awakening* or *Enlightenment*?

26. Which of the Doctor's famous foes were sometimes affected by lightwave sickness?

27. The second Doctor regenerated at the end of which story: *The War Games, The Krotons, The Mind Robber*?

28. In *The Gunfighters*, what alias does the Doctor give himself?

29. In the first series of *Doctor Who*, was Ian Chesterton: a science teacher, a maths teacher, a geography teacher or a history teacher?

30. On the planet, Marinus, what was the name of the hostile creatures, beginning with the letter V?

31. Who was the Chancellor of Peladon: Torbis, Peladon or Izlyr?

32. In *Vengeance on Varos*, what sort of creature does Peri turn into under cell mutation: a frog, a bird, a cat or a snake?

33. Did Chessene and the Sontarans make an appearance in: *The Leisure Hive, The Two Doctors* or *The Curse of Fenric*?

34. In *Trial of a Time Lord*, what is the name of the Doctor's prosecutor, beginning with the letter V?

35. Actress Jean Marsh played three different characters in the *Doctor Who* TV show. In real life, which *Doctor Who* actor was she once married to?

36. In *The Android Invasion*, who is in charge of UNIT while the Brigadier is in Geneva: Sergeant Benton, Captain Yates or Colonel Faraday?

37. In *Vengeance on Varos*, what is the title given to the leader elected by the 1,620,783 voters of Varos?

38. In *The Pirate Planet*, who kills the Captain: Queen Xanxia, the Mentiads or the Doctor?

39. In *The Robots of Death*, D84 is an ally of: government agent Poul, the Master or Taren Capel?

40. Which story features the Doctor and his companions in France during the sixteenth century: *The Massacre, The Time Meddler* or *The Time Warrior*?

41. In *Planet of Giants*, the pesticide capable of killing all insects is: IS9, DN6, OP4 or LV7?

42. In *Attack of the Cybermen*, who is killed when helping the Doctor destroy the Cyber Controller: Lytton, Peri, Morgus or Adric?

43. What is the nickname of the commune in *The Green Death*: the Nut Hutch, the Long Hair Home, the Hippie Hovel or the Madhouse?

44. In *The Brain of Morbius*, who was tried by the Time Lords and vapourised?

45. In *The Savages*, who is the leader of the Council of Elders: Jano, Krystos or Vannevar?

46. In *Horror of Fang Rock*, Lord Palmerdale's secretary has the same name as an Australian city. What is it?

47. In *Dragonfire*, what is the name of the exiled criminal whose ice-cold touch kills and who has a wife called Xana?

48. Which *Doctor Who* companion was originally a sailor in the British Navy on the ship, HMS Teazer?

49. Which *Doctor Who* story received the lowest British viewing figures?

50. Famous comedy actor, Geoffrey Palmer, who appeared in *Reginald Perrin* and *Butterflies*, played how many different characters in *Doctor Who*: one, two or three?

1. Which of the Doctor's adversaries does he save from death in *The Time Monster*?

2. Which *Doctor Who* story saw both Jamie and Zoe leave the Doctor?

3. Can you name either of the people who sabotage the Source in *The Keeper of Traken* in order to destroy the Master's TARDIS?

4. In *Delta and the Bannermen*, what purple-coloured creatures arrive on Earth as tourists?

5. Albert Ward was a stunt double only used to replicate what part of the Doctor's body?

6. Does the Doctor kill the Mykra with: an ultra-violet converter, a sonic screwdriver, a radiation scanner or a converted missile?

7. What is the name of the 15-year-old girl character in the first episodes of *Doctor Who*?

8. In *The Tenth Planet*, Ben and others hold uranium rods to ward off which frequent enemies of the Doctor?

9. Which comedian, who appeared in *The Young Ones*, played the role of a DJ in *Revelation of the Daleks*?

10. Which companion does the Doctor take back to her home in Hillview Road, Croyden, before journeying on to Gallifrey?

11. Which *Doctor Who* actor died in 1987 whilst attending a *Doctor Who* convention in the United States?

12. Some of what creatures in *The Green Death* were made by the special effects teams from inflated condoms?

13. What is the two-word name of the facility on the planet, Necros, where bodies can be cryogenically frozen?

14. In *Spearhead from Space*, what vehicle owned by Dr Beavis does the Doctor steal?

15. Who programmed the Robots of Death to kill?

16. If you were watching Cybermen invade the South Pole Space Tracking Station, would you be viewing an episode featuring: the first Doctor, the third Doctor or the fifth Doctor?

17. The fourth segment of the Key to Time is disguised as: part of a statue, a crossbow, an android or a wax seal?

18. In *The Seeds of Doom*, did Doctor Who disguise himself as: a cleaner, a chauffeur or a security guard?

19. In which story featuring the seventh Doctor did jazz musician, Courtney Pine, and his band appear as themselves?

20. Before Peter Purves was cast as one of Doctor Who's companions, what other character had he played in the show: Morton Dill, a Cyberman or the Master?

21. In *The Enemy of the World*, what is the name of the world leader, born in Mexico, who has developed a sun store which will put an end to famine?

22. Which segment of the Key to Time is actually a person?

23. In *Planet of the Daleks*, what is the name of the plain on the planet, Spiridon, to which all creatures travel at night to keep warm?

24. Can you name the two stories in which the shape-shifting character Kamelion physically appears?

25. Which *Doctor Who* story is located in Tombstone, in the days of the Wild West?

26. In *The Evil of the Daleks*, the Daleks use Theodore Maxtible's time cabinet. How many mirrors does it have: 72, 144 or 256?

27. Who was fattened up by the cannibals, Tabby and Tilda, and attacked with a toasting fork: Peri, Jo Grant or Melanie Bush?

28. Which one of the following is not a location through which the Daleks chase the Doctor: the *Marie Celeste* ship, the planet Xeros, the Empire State Building or the planet Aridius?

29. In *The Armageddon Factor*, the Shadow works for: the Master, the Daleks, the Black Guardian or Drax?

30. When the third Doctor is avoiding an attempt to kidnap him from Ashbridge Cottage Hospital, what does he use as an escape vehicle?

31. In *Planet of Evil*, which professor is turned into Anti-Man by an antimatter infection?

32. In project 'Inferno', what colour is the fluid from the drilling pipes which infects humans?

33. Which *Doctor Who* companion came from Pease Pottage, Sussex?

34. What is the real identity of the planet, Ravolox, revealed eventually to the sixth Doctor?

35. Which robotic creature was controlled by a silver sphere buried deep within its chest?

36. The Visians live on planet: Mira, Kembel or Skaro?

37. In *The Invisible Enemy*, what is the name of the foundation the Doctor heads to after he is infected by an alien virus?

38. What was the name of the antique car driven by the third Doctor?

39. In which story featuring the fourth Doctor do viewers learn that the Master has used up all twelve of his regenerations?

40. The statue in *Silver Nemesis* is made of what living metal?

41. In *The Mark of the Rani*, what do people who step on the Rani's mines turn into?

42. In *Attack of the Cybermen*, the Cybermen hid their time vessel on what body in the solar system?

43. In *Terror of the Autons*, what type of flower do the Nestenes create to spray a suffocating film over humans?

44. In *The Caves of Androzani*, who falls in love with the Doctor's companion, Peri?

45. Which of the following stories did not appear in the last season of the seventh Doctor: *The Curse of Fenric, The Happiness Patrol* or *Ghost Light*?

46. In *Planet of the Daleks*, a group of creatures are on a mission to stop the Daleks, led by their commander, Miro, and their ship's doctor, Taron. Who are they?

47. Who feeds Keeler raw meat to speed up his changing into a Krynoid?

48. In *The Rescue*, what was the name of the planet the Doctor travelled to: Terra Alpha, Vaxos, Dido or Gallifrey?

49. What colour was the trim on the fifth Doctor's beige jacket?

50. In *Day of the Daleks*, is Dalakanium: a metal, an explosive or a medicine?

1. What does Ace frequently call the seventh Doctor: Sir, Doc, Genius or Professor?

2. Manesha was the best friend of which *Doctor Who* companion: Ace, Nyssa, Romana or Leela?

3. In *The Masque of Mandragora*, which combat technique does the Doctor use on Sarah's kidnapper: Venusian boxing, aikido or karate?

4. What is the only story in which the fourth Doctor does not wear his trademark scarf?

5. What is the name of the first story to feature Zoe Heriot as a companion of the Doctor?

6. Who were the original inhabitants of Earth: the Silurians, the Axons or the Sea Devils?

7. No master copy exists of *The Tomb of the Cybermen* in the BBC archives: true or false?

8. Well-known actor, Philip Madoc, played the War Lord in *The War Games*. But which role did he play in *The Brain of Morbius*?

9. The spaceship which brought Josiah Samuel Smith to Earth was made from what material?

10. In *Mawdryn Undead*, how many years have Mawdryn and his band of mutants been travelling in a space liner for: 500, 1,000, 2,000 or 3,000 years?

11. In *The Happiness Patrol*, what was the name of the planet on which sadness is illegal?

12. In *The Smugglers*, which of Captain Pike's arms ends with a hook?

13. Which *Doctor Who* story, never completed, was partly used in *The Five Doctors*?

14. Who was the first intruder to operate the TARDIS: Salamander, Davros, the Cyber Controller or Kelig?

15. Which planet features a monster called Aggredor, a high priest called Hepesh and a chancellor called Torbis: Peladon, Trion or Terra Alpha?

16. Which famous science fiction writer accompanies the Doctor in *Timelash*?

17. In *Planet of the Spiders*, the third Doctor says he learned how to compress his muscles from which famous Earth escapologist?

18. In which story does the Doctor take part in a cricket match due to a case of mistaken identity: *Kinda, Black Orchid*, or *Earthshock*?

19. Commander Lytton appears in *Attack of the Cybermen*, but he was first seen working for which other adversaries of Doctor Who?

20. Which *Doctor Who* companion was the daughter of the Counsel Tremas?

21. In *Kinda*, who becomes possessed by a Mara: Adric, Nyssa or Tegan?

22. In *The Moonbase*, the Cybermen had undergone a re-design. Their fingers were replaced with claws – but how many were on each hand?

23. Which *Doctor Who* enemy fires a mist containing ultra-sharp fragments and feeds off of mind power?

24. In which European country is part of *The Two Doctors* set?

25. In the very first *Doctor Who* story, what was the name of Za's rival for leadership of the tribe?

26. The Kraal Virus featured in which story: *The Face of Evil, The Ice Warriors, The Android Invasion* or *Terror of the Zygons*?

27. In *Paradise Towers*, are Kangs: robotic cleaners who kill, the name given to the caretakers or gangs of girls?

28. If you were watching *Attack of the Cybermen*, which Doctor would you be viewing in action: the second, fourth or sixth?

29. Campbell Singer played three roles in *The Celestial Toymaker*. Which one of the following was not one of them: Sergeant Rugg, Joey, King of Hearts, Cyril?

30. In *Terminus*, what was the name of the enormous spacecraft located at the centre of the universe which has been turned into a hospital?

31. In *The Ark in Space*, what is the biblical name of the leader of the crew?

32. The sixth Doctor meets a chemistry genius who was exiled by the Time Lords for turning mice into monsters. What is this genius's name?

33. What was the name of Adric's brother, who sacrificed his own life?

34. What household substance, loaded into shotgun cartridges, is used to destroy the Fendahleen?

35. At the start of *Ghost Light*, what Victorian toy did the Doctor climb on within moments of leaving the TARDIS?

36. In *The Seeds of Death*, who is the only character to be hit directly by a seed pod and survive?

37. What is a T-Mat: a form of travel, a robot ally of the Cybermen or a planet?

38. In *The Aztecs*, which Doctor accidentally proposes marriage to Cameca?

39. What was the name of Professor Brett's secretary, who became a companion of the Doctor's?

40. Which Doctor is short-sighted in his right eye: the third, fifth or seventh?

41. *The Gunfighters* featured characters played by actors who provided the voices of Scott Tracy and Brains in *Thunderbirds*: true or false?

42. In *The Three Doctors*, who enlisted the Doctor's help because a black hole was draining their energy forces?

43. In *The Leisure Hive*, what colour was the triangle worn by Pangol the Argolin around his neck?

44. What is the name of the first story to feature the second Doctor?

45. What was the hundredth *Doctor Who* story: *The Stones of Blood, The Pirate Planet* or *Spearhead from Space*?

46. In *The Crusade*, which of the Doctor's companions is kidnapped by El Akir?

47. Which companion of the Doctor meets her double, called Ann Talbot, in *Black Orchid*?

48. In *Dragonfire*, who takes over the management of Iceworld in the story after Kane dies?

49. In *Ghost Light*, how much money does Josiah Smith offer the Doctor to tackle his enemy: £50, £500, £5,000 or £5,000,000?

50. In *Paradise Towers*, which one of the following was not a member of the Red Kangs: Exit, Fire Escape, Bin Liner, Air Duct?

1. In *The War Machines*, who does the Doctor hypnotise to reverse the effects of WOTAN?

2. In *Day of the Daleks* and *Frontier in Space*, what colour is the leader of the Daleks?

3. Who offers to sacrifice themselves to the Daemon instead of the Doctor, causing the Daemon to self-destruct?

4. Who does Leela fall in love with in *The Invasion of Time*?

5. In *Horror of Fang Rock*, the Doctor destroys the Rutan by firing which of Lord Palmerdale's precious objects: diamonds, gold sovereigns or Cuban cigars?

6. In *The Smugglers*, who hid Pirate Avery's treasure: 'Holy' Joe Longfoot, Zeb Gurney or Daniel Smallbeer?

7. Who is asked by Chal to lead the two conflicting races in *The Savages*?

8. In *Terror of the Autons*, whose TARDIS turns into a horsebox?

9. How many rows of half-spheres did the original Daleks have on their bodies?

10. Theta Sigma is a name used for which character in the show?

11. In *Spearhead from Space*, meteorites flying in formation and containing the Nestene Consciousness landed on which planet?

12. Which official on Traken summons the Doctor to identify and combat evil?

13. In which decade of the twentieth century is *The Abominable Snowmen* set?

14. On what planet are its inhabitants divided between those who worship the fire god, Logar, and those who don't?

15. The leader of the Outlers on Alzarius is the brother of a Doctor's companion. Can you name him?

16. In *Inferno*, when the Doctor travels to the alternate world, what is the name of the UNIT-like organisation in charge of security there?

17. Borusa was once the Doctor's: servant, tutor, employer or pet?

18. Is Skaro the seventh, ninth, twelfth or fifteenth planet in its solar system?

19. In *The Ribos Operation*, what colour is the rarest element in the galaxy, jethrik stone?

20. Who seeks to gain control of Kronos using a device known as TOMTIT?

21. In *Image of the Fendahl*, the Fendahl lay dormant inside an item which was millions of years old. What was this?

22. In *Robot*, which robot goes mad when it kills its creator by accident?

23. Which early *Doctor Who* companion has a fight to the death with the Aztec warrior, Ixta?

24. What was the name of the underground people who were the original inhabitants of Terra Alpha?

25. What was the name of the double of the Doctor in *The Enemy of the World*?

26. The actress who played Servalan in *Blake's 7* also played Chessene in *The Two Doctors*. What was her name?

27. Who scores more than any of the Gonds on the Teaching Machine: Zoe, Jamie or K-9?

28. One of the four *Doctor Who* writers for the 2004 series is a member of which popular comedy team: *The League of Gentlemen*, *Little Britain* or *Dead Ringers*?

29. In *Silver Nemesis*, what is the name of the Nazi, played by Anton Diffring, who has custody of the bow from the Nemesis statue?

30. What colour was the third Doctor's beloved antique car?

31. Which *Doctor Who* actor previously appeared in *Blake's 7* and *The Brothers*?

32. How many times has the word 'death' been a part of a *Doctor Who* story title: three times, five times, seven times or nine times?

33. In *The Robots of Death*, what gas is used to raise the pitch of Taren Capel's voice, so that his voice commands are not recognised by his robots?

34. Which air hostess entered the TARDIS thinking it was a police telephone box and became a companion of the Doctor?

35. What is the name of the one-eyed servants found on the Ark: Cylcoids, Monoids or Unoids?

36. In *Underworld*, what is the Oracle which guards the Minyan's race bank: a multi-tentacled monster, a force field, a computer or a giant dog?

37. The Gods of Ragnarok turn out to be the only family in attendance at what entertainment facility?

38. Which Blue Peter presenter appeared in *Attack of the Cybermen*?

39. Liz Shaw becomes a companion of the third Doctor. Is she an expert in: alien life forms, meteorites, solar energy or atomic weaponry?

40. The first ever episode of *Doctor Who* featured the Doctor recovering from a hangover: true or false?

41. In *The Daleks' Master Plan*, which companion of the Doctor is tricked into killing her own brother, Bret Vyon?

42. In *The Mutants*, who kills the Marshal: Varan, Ky, Jo or the Doctor?

43. Who is in charge of the Antarctic base station in *The Tenth Planet*?

44. Sergeant Benton of UNIT retires from the force to: bring up his daughter, run a second-hand car dealership or become a teacher?

45. In *The Sun Makers,* what planet are Earth people now living on?

46. Which Beatrix Potter story does K-9 read in *The Creature From The Pit*?

47. In *The Space Pirates*, what item does the Doctor use to open an audio lock?

48. Who played the Doctor in *The War Games*?

49. In *The Invasion*, what is the name of the company run by Tobias Vaughan?

50. On what planet did the Doctor first meet Adric?

QUIZ 17

1. Did Christopher Eccleston or David Tennant star as the Doctor in *Boom Town*?

2. In *The Christmas Invasion*, is Torchwood, Ultrabeam or Firestorm the code name of the particle beam fired by the British Prime Minister?

3. In *Fear Her*, are there one, three, five or thirteen Isolus on Earth?

4. Who was Rose Tyler's boyfriend at the start of the first new series?

5. Which con man is rescued by the TARDIS at the end of *The Doctor Dances*?

6. Do potions based on mistletoe, hemlock, garlic or arsenic repel the werewolf in *Tooth and Claw*?

7. In *Aliens of London*, what London landmark does the alien spacecraft crash into on its way to landing in the River Thames?

8. Who is with Rose in *Doomsday* when the Daleks absorb information from Dr Singh, killing him in the process?

9. Which Duke is cured by Matron Casp in *New Earth*?

10. In *Fear Her*, what item does Rose throw the Isolus pod at to give the pod heat?

11. In *The Unquiet Dead* which famous writer accompanies the Doctor and Rose to the TARDIS?

12. What item of Victor Kennedy's in *Love & Monsters* does Elton snap in half to make the alien absorb into the Earth?

13. In *The End of the World*, does the Moxx of Balhoon, the Face of Boe or Jabe give the Doctor and Rose a cutting of her grandfather?

14. What is the name of the South London estate that Jackie Tyler lives on in *Army of Ghosts*?

15. In *The Empty Child*, does Constantine tell the Doctor that Nancy's brother, Jamie, was taken to Room 191, 406, 777 or 802?

16. In *The Christmas Invasion*, is the Guinevere One probe sent to explore Mars, Gallifrey or Vortis?

17. Henry van Statten calls the one living alien in his collection a Cybernet, a Metaltron or a Slitherfish?

18. In *Tooth and Claw*, is the name of the servant who hides in Rose's closet Victoria, Isobel or Flora?

19. Who, in *Aliens of London*, calls the alien emergency number to tip off the authorities about the Doctor?

20. In *Rose*, what device does the Doctor use to 'disarm' the hostile mannequin's arm in Rose and Jackie's flat?

21. Does a Dalek, Cyberman or Slitheen emerge from the black sphere in *Army of Ghosts*?

22. Did the alien 'bomb' that set off the zombie humans in *The Empty Child* and *The Doctor Dances* land at Lime Street, Waterloo, Kings Cross or Euston railway station?

23. In *The Idiot's Lantern*, what did the Doctor and Rose use as transport in the 1950s?

24. In *Tooth and Claw*, into what device does the Doctor insert the Koh-i-noor diamond to create a weapon to destroy the werewolf?

25. In *The Empty Child*, what is the name of the girl who steals food during the Blitz?

26. How many million Cybermen have landed on Earth in *Doomsday*?

27. Does the Doctor advise van Statten's men to fire at the eyepiece, the brain cortex or the base of the Dalek?

28. Who travels high above London in *The Empty Child* holding onto the rope of a floating balloon?

29. In *The Satan's Pit*, who uses a bolt firer to smash the rocket's shield, releasing Toby into space to help kill the beast?

30. In *Boom Town*, what is the human name of the last surviving member of the Slitheen, now the mayoress of a city?

31. What story does Doctor Who congratulate Charles Dickens for writing in *The Unquiet Dead*?

32. What is the name of the girl in *Love & Monsters* who ends up as a face in a paving stone?

33. Does the Doctor accompany Ida, Toby, Zak or Jefferson onto the planet in *The Satan Pit*?

34. In *Army of Ghosts* the Doctor pretends his companion is Jackie Tyler when he is held at gunpoint inside which institute?

35. What is the first name of the child in *School Reunion*, who answers all of the Doctor's questions in his first lesson as a teacher?

36. What is K9's first word to the Doctor after it is repaired in the episode, *School Reunion*?

37. In *The Unquiet Dead*, whose grandmother is the first of the dead to rise?

38. Riding what animal does the Doctor leap through the window of the palace in *The Girl in the Fireplace*?

39. Is Wilson, Jackson or Henderson the name of the chief electrician Rose goes into the basement of the department store to search for in the very first episode of the new series?

40. What is the name of the girl in *Fear Her* who has been infiltrated by the Isolus and constantly draws?

41. In *Rose*, the first time we see Rose, what time is shown on her alarm clock?

42. In *The Parting of the Ways*, does the Doctor, Rose or Jackie borrow a repair truck from Rodrigo to help open up the TARDIS?

43. In *Bad Wolf*, who was the first *Weakest Link* contestant to be disintegrated?

44. In *The End of the World*, which lady does the Doctor reverse teleport back to Platform One where she dries out and dies?

45. Who is the first *Big Brother* contestant to be voted out of the house containing the Doctor in *Bad Wolf*?

46. In *The End of the World*, does the TARDIS take Rose and the Doctor three, five, seven or nine billion years into the future?

47. In *Rose*, what is the first name of the website owner Rose visits to learn about The Doctor?

48. In *Boom Town*, what is the name of Mickey's new girlfriend, who he tells Rose about?

49. In *The Long Game*, Suki turns out to be a freedom fighter. What is her real name?

50. In *The End of the World*, Lady Cassandra's Earth gift is a jukebox she calls an iPod. What song is first played on it and by which artist?

QUIZ 18

1. Which *Doctor Who* companion used poisonous Janus thorns to get herself out of danger?

2. In *Inferno*, who helps the Doctor to use fire extinguishers to kill Stahlman?

3. In *Attack of the Cybermen*, which three of the following does the TARDIS turn into: table, gate, organ, tree, cabinet, London bus?

4. The Daleks' former selves, the Kaleds, fought with which race?

5. Which planet in the Earth's solar system is the only one to contain Taranium?

6. In *The Time Monster*, the Doctor manages to materialise his own TARDIS inside whose TARDIS?

7. In *Day of the Daleks,* the Doctor and which companion meet themselves?

8. Which character, encountered by the Doctor in *Trial of a Time Lord*, does he meet again in *Dragonfire*?

9. In *The Underwater Menace*, what is the name of the goddess worshipped in Atlantis: Amdo, Amphibia, Gillio or Reptilius?

10. Which former writer and script editor on *Doctor Who* went on to create characters such as Arthur Dent and Ford Prefect, in books, radio and television?

11. Which actress and wife of Ryder Cup golf captain, Sam Torrance, appeared as Agella in *Destiny of the Daleks*?

12. Which Doctor wore a panama hat and a golf jumper covered in question marks?

13. In which story does Kronos destroy Atlantis?

14. In *Warriors of the Deep*, how many limbs did the Myrka have?

15. The Zero Room is used by Time Lords to: imprison mortal enemies, to communicate with the dead or to heal after a tough regeneration?

16. Which companion of the Doctor's is found to be suffering from Spectrox Toxaemia?

17. Which famous female children's author was approached to write an episode for the 2004 *Doctor Who* series but turned it down?

18. Alzarius is the home of which swamp-living creature?

19. In *Carnival of Monsters*, which frequent foe of the Doctor is found in the miniscope: the Master, Daleks or Cybermen?

20. Which *Doctor Who* actor died in 1975?

21. Which actor played the Doctor in *The Curse of Fenric*?

22. In *The Deadly Assassin*, what is the Master's TARDIS disguised as: a grandfather clock, the Rod of Rassilon or a wooden chest?

23. In both *The Talons of Weng-Chiang* and *The Invasion of Time*, the Doctor whistles the theme tune from which famous war film starring Alec Guinness?

24. In *Frontier in Space*, who saves the Doctor from the Daleks?

25. In *Timelash*, what was the name of the ruler of Karfel, beginning with the letter B?

26. In *The Five Doctors*, Chancellor Flavia asks the Doctor to stay on which planet to perform his work as Lord President?

27. Are the people on the planet, Chloris, short of: water, metal, plants or salt?

28. In *The Hand of Fear*, the Doctor punches one of his companions. Who is it?

29. How many bleeps does a Quark robot give to confirm an order?

30. In *The Curse of Fenric*, Baby Audrey turns out to be the mother of which companion of the Doctor's?

31. In *City of Death*, which Shakespeare play does the Doctor say he wrote the first draft?

32. In *Nightmare of Eden*, which two of the following are ships locked together: Empress, Sandminer, Nerva, Hecate?

33. In *The Dalek Invasion of Earth*, what is the alternative name of the Black Dalek?

34. What weapon in the shape of a small black rod can transform a human body into the size of a doll?

35. In which *Doctor Who* story would you find Harrison Chase?

36. The Inquisitor tells the Doctor that a Krontep warlord has married Peri. What is his name?

37. How does the Kandyman kill his victims: by crushing their spines, drowning them or electrocuting them?

38. Who is the leader of the savages in the *Doctor Who* story of the same name: Chal, Senta or Jano?

39. Who does the Doctor poison with cyanide in *The Two Doctors*?

40. Which companion of the Doctor manages to subdue the Aztec warrior, Ixta, with a nerve pinch to the neck?

41. Which Doctor was forced to regenerate after suffering a dose of blue radiation from the planet, Metebelis 3?

42. In *Pyramids of Mars*, who imprisoned Sutekh under a pyramid with a force field?

43. Which *Doctor Who* actor was born James Kent-Smith?

44. In the *Robots of Death*, which one of the following was not a crew member of the Sandminer: Toos, Graff, Poul, Uvanov?

45. In *The Space Pirates*, what is the name of the mining prospector and commander of the C-class ship LIZ 79?

46. In *The Daleks' Master Plan*, whose directional unit does the Doctor steal?

47. In *The Faceless Ones*, which TARDIS traveller witnesses a murder in an aircraft hanger and then disappears?

48. Which of the Doctor's companions was taken over by the computer, WOTAN?

49. In *Doctor Who: The Movie*, the spirit of the Master took over the body of a driver of what sort of vehicle?

50. In *Battlefield*, what was the name of the mother of Mordred?

1. What colour leather jacket did the Doctor played by Christopher Eccleston wear?

2. Did the Daleks, the Cybermen or the Time Lords build the Genesis Ark?

3. In *The Parting of the Ways*, how many Daleks does Anne Droid destroy before she is destroyed?

4. The TARDIS reverses the Slitheen's life so that it becomes a microchip, a vial of liquid, an egg or a grain of sand?

5. Is Emily, Julia or Gwyneth the servant girl the Doctor uses as a medium to contact the aliens in *The Unquiet Dead*?

6. Which member of the space station in *The Impossible Planet* dies first: Scooter, Ida Scott or Mr Jefferson?

7. The Doctor is summoned to a giant hospital by the Face of Boe in: *New Earth*, *The Satan Pit*, *Boom Town* or *The End of the World*?

8. In *The Doctor Dances*, the Doctor says that the weapons factories of Villengard have been turned into: a banana grove, a hospital, a children's park or a prison?

9. In *Boom Town*, in which British city is the giant nuclear reactor being built under orders by the Slitheen mayoress?

10. In *The End of the World*, does the Doctor use a mind control bracelet, psychic paper or bribery to convince the Steward that they are invited guests on Platform One?

11. In *Dalek*, is Paul, Adam or Steven the name of the English employee of van Statten's who travels in the TARDIS with Rose and the Doctor at the end of the episode?

12. Which character, first seen in *The End of the World*, announces in *The Long Game* that he is pregnant?

13. Is Eddie Connolly, Mr Magpie or Rita Connolly the person informing the police about the faceless humans in *The Idiot's Lantern*?

14. In *Father's Day*, in what building did Rose, the Doctor and Rose's mother and father shelter from the flying aliens?

15. In *The Christmas Invasion*, is Danny Llewellyn, Jackie Tyler or Major Blake in charge of the Guinevere project?

16. What subject is Martha Jones studying?

17. In *The Unquiet Dead*, does Charles Dickens fill the room with water, gas or soldiers to keep the Gelth at bay?

18. In the parallel universe that Jake takes the Doctor to in *Doomsday*, which parallel member of Rose's family does the Doctor meet?

19. In *Rose*, Clive shows Rose a picture of the Doctor in the crowd in front of the motorcade of which US President?

20. In *Bad Wolf*, which Asian country had the Doctor just escaped from when the trans mat beamed him into *Big Brother*?

21. Is Captain Jack trying to sell a Slitheen, Dalek, Vortis or Chula spaceship when he mistakes Rose for a Time Agent?

22. In *World War Three*, who throws vinegar from a jar of pickled eggs to destroy one of the Slitheen?

23. Which M.P. in *Aliens of London* observes the acting Prime Minister and his advisors break wind loudly then remove their human heads?

24. The Doctor tells the Daleks that his nickname in Dalek history is: 'The Vengeful One', 'The Oncoming Storm' or 'The Dark Lord'?

25. The Doctor and Rose watch which TV soap show featuring one of the army of ghosts?

26. What item of Jackie Tyler's does she find in Elton Pope's jacket pocket in *Love & Monsters*?

27. Where does Rose find the Isolus pod spaceship in *Fear Her*?

28. In *World War Three*, what item does the Doctor use on the Slitheen in order to rescue Harriet and Rose?

29. Is Lady Cassandra, the Moxx of Balhoon or the Face of Boe responsible for tampering with the gravity shields on Platform One?

30. Whose underground bunker do the Doctor and Rose land in at the start of *Dalek*?

31. How long does the Doctor say it will take him to build a machine to create a delta wave to wipe out the Daleks: 40 minutes, six hours, three days or a week?

32. What is the name of the character in the television in *The Idiot's Lantern* who sucks Rose's face into the TV?

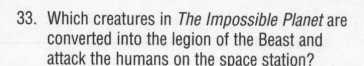

33. Which creatures in *The Impossible Planet* are converted into the legion of the Beast and attack the humans on the space station?

34. What girl's name in *Love & Monsters* is the abbreviated name of the group of Doctor Who enthusiasts?

35. In which country do Rose and the Doctor meet right at the end of the second series?

36. In *School Reunion*, what is the human name of the headmaster played by Anthony Head who turns out to be the leader of the Krillitanes?

37. Who rescues Rose from the Blitz using his spacecraft's tractor beam in *The Empty Child*?

38. At the very start of *Aliens of London*, how many months is it since Rose's mum has seen Rose?

39. In *The End of the World*, the Repeated Meme give egg-shaped gifts which reveal what sort of metallic creature?

40. In *School Reunion*, what is the name of the school in which the Doctor confronts the Krillitanes?

41. What is the name of the department store that Rose worked in before meeting the Doctor?

42. In *The Girl in the Fireplace*, which French king watches the hearse carrying Reinette pull away?

43. In *Tooth and Claw*, which band did the Doctor promise to take Rose to see in London in 1979?

44. Who lights a match, killing herself but destroying the rift in *The Unquiet Dead*?

45. In *World War Three* what is the password into the UNIT website that the Doctor gives Mickey?

46. At the start *The Long Game*, what food item is the Doctor told costs Two Credits Twenty?

47. In *The Satan Pit*, what is the number of the security strategy the commander of the space station orders?

48. What is the name in English of the coastal bay in which Rose and the Doctor finally say goodbye at the end of the second new series?

49. What is the registration number of Mickey Smith's yellow car?

50. In *Love & Monsters*, what ELO song are Elton Pope and the others playing in their newly formed band when Victor Kennedy walks in?

DIFFICULT QUIZ

1. In the first episode of *Doctor Who*, what is the name of the road on which the junkyard is situated?

2. What is Romana's full name?

3. What metal, found on Mogar, does the sixth Doctor use to kill the Vervoids?

4. In *Frontier in Space*, what does the Doctor places his hands on to send telepathic messages to the Time Lords?

5. In *Paradise Towers*, what word, beginning with the letter W, is given to graffiti?

6. In *The Greatest Show in the Galaxy*, which explorer always carries special tea with him, which the Doctor identifies as coming from Melagophon?

7. In *The Green Death*, what was the full name of the BOSS computer?

8. In *The Happiness Patrol* and *The Armageddon Factor*, there are mentions of the Doctor's nickname when he was at college. What is it?

9. What was the name of Steven Taylor's panda mascot?

10. Two fourth Doctor stories with the word 'death' in their title achieved the two largest British TV audience ratings. What were they?

11. In *The Stones of Blood*, what is the full name of the establishment known by its initials, BIDS?

12. Which one of the Eternals in *Enlightenment* cured Tegan of her seasickness?

13. What is the name of the chairman of the Sirius Conglomerate on Androzani Minor?

14. In *The Curse of Peladon*, whe Doctor sings a Venusian lullaby to calm Aggredor – but on what English hymn is the tune based?

15. What is the name of Sarah Jane Smith's aunt, who was a renowned virologist?

16. The fifth Doctor carries a vegetable to warn him of deadly gases – but what does he do with it if the gases are present?

17. What is the full name of the WOTAN computer?

18. In *Nightmare of Eden*, what does CET stand for in CET Machine?

19. Which member of UNIT is a keen ballroom dancer?

20. Who did the Black Guardian choose to influence the Eternals race across the solar system?

21. Midge and Squeak were siblings in which *Doctor Who* story?

22. In *The Tenth Planet*, what was the name of the rocket on which a Z-bomb was mounted?

23. In *The Face of Evil*, the only entrance in the Black Wall is where on the cliff?

24. In *The Seeds of Death*, what is the name of the minister with special responsibility for T-Mat?

25. In *The Smugglers*, which one of the crew of the Black Albatross had a wooden leg?

26. In *Warriors of the Deep*, what is the name of the last of the Silurian Triad?

27. In *The Master*, the Master was shrunk in size to how many inches high?

28. What is the name of the planet in *The Horns Of Nimon*, run by Soldeed, which was once the centre of a huge empire?

29. By what other name is Kingpin known in *The Greatest Show in the Galaxy*?

30. In *Ghost Light*, what is the name of the program activated by light which is set to cause an explosion?

31. In *Carnival of Monsters*, what planet do Jo and the Doctor arrive upon concealed in a miniscope?

32. What is name of the nerve agent which the Cybermen use to contaminate the food of the Moonbase colonists?

33. What creature has destroyed the Wheel's supplies of Bernalium?

34. In *Inferno*, what is the name of the maintenance worker infected by the slime from the output pipes, who turns insane and kills someone?

35. In *The Space Pirates*, what is the name of the planet which the pirates are sending parts of the space beacons to?

36. In *Revenge of the Cybermen*, a plague created by the Cybermen has reduced the living occupants of Nerva Beacon from 50 to how many?

37. In *The Sontaran Experiment*, what is Sontaran, Field Major Styre, performing experiments on?

38. What is the name of the magazine Sarah Jane Smith works as a reporter for?

39. In *The Time Warrior*, what is the name of the Sontaran who kidnaps twentieth century scientists to help repair his spaceship?

40. What is the name of the Time Lord Chancellor who works with the Master in *The Deadly Assassin*?

41. What was held for the first time in 1977 in a church hall in Clapham in London?

42. In *The Stones of Blood*, what is the name of the stone circle in which the third segment of the Key to Time is to be found?

43. In *Frontios*, the Gravis led which group of slug-like creatures?

44. What was the name of the robot which killed a group of Cybermen in *The Five Doctors*?

45. What was the name of the first person to die on Argolis, being torn apart in the Tachyon Recreation Generator?

46. In *Battlefield*, what is the name of the female Brigadier in charge of all or part of UNIT?

47. In *The Happiness Patrol*, what is the name of the official from the Galactic Census Bureau?

48. Whose boyfriend, Billy, falls in love with Delta and mutates into a Chimeron in order to leave Earth with her?

49. What is the full name of the Master's invention known by the abbreviation, TOMTIT?

50. In *Spearhead from Space*, what is the registration of the red antique car the Doctor steals to escape from Ashbridge College Hospital?

ANSWERS

1. The TARDIS
2. The Time Lords
3. The third Doctor
4. Regeneration
5. Christopher Eccleston
6. Two
7. K-9
8. Jon Pertwee
9. The TARDIS
10. Billie Piper

11. A scarf
12. A telephone box
13. The Daleks
14. Leslie Grantham
15. The Daleks
16. Peter Davison
17. The seventh Doctor
18. Patrick Troughton
19. Gold
20. Sarah Jane Smith

21. Peter Purves
22. The Daleks
23. BBC Cardiff
24. Mars
25. The Cybermen

26. Gallifrey
27. Mathematicians
28. Matthew Corbett
29. Missile-firing tail
30. The third Doctor

31. William Hartnell
32. Bagpipes
33. Bernard Bresslaw
34. *The War of the Worlds*
35. Rose
36. Jon Pertwee
37. Zeus
38. Peri
39. Gatwick airport
40. William Hartnell

41. The Master
42. Ace
43. The sixth Doctor
44. His knee
45. Peter Davison
46. Space Station Camera
47. Tom Baker
48. Blue
49. Cyanide
50. Seventh

QUIZ 1

1. Peri
2. *Doctor Who and the Silurians*
3. A vegetarian
4. Malkon
5. He is the Master in disguise
6. Barbara Wright
7. The Navy
8. *Ghost Light*
9. 40 years
10. Ron Grainer

11. Elizabeth 'Liz' Shaw
12. Professor Sorenson
13. Lemonade
14. Svartos
15. Magnus Greel
16. Tom Baker and Lalla Ward
17. A spear
18. Harry
19. Sensorites
20. Vulcan

21. Radiation
22. Jo Grant
23. The sixth Doctor
24. Vortis
25. Mickey

26. Radiation
27. The Thals
28. Senex
29. The Master
30. Alistair, Gordon

31. *The Time Warrior*
32. Mondas
33. *The Smugglers*
34. Ruth
35. Seabase Four
36. The Hundred Years War zone
37. Devil's End
38. Harold Pinter
39. Perivale
40. The Great Intelligence

41. Nimrod
42. Seven
43. William Hartnell
44. Earth
45. The second Doctor
46. *Arc of Infinity, The Deadly Assassin, The Five Doctors, The Invasion of Time*
47. Harrogate
48. Oracle
49. The Time Vector Generator
50. Twenty-second century

QUIZ 2

1. Nyssa and Tegan
2. Ian Chesterton
3. Amsterdam
4. Sarah Jane Smith
5. An asteroid
6. *Resurrection of the Daleks Part II*
7. *Genesis of the Daleks*
8. Tom Baker

9. Omega
10. *The Four Doctors*

11. Tegan
12. Kronos
13. The United States
14. One
15. WOTAN
16. Third Doctor
17. Caven
18. *The Myth Makers*
19. The Master
20. The mine

21. The sixth Doctor
22. 500 years
23. Commander Andred
24. The Master
25. The Black Guardian
26. Three times
27. Kroll
28. *The Dalek Invasion of Earth*
29. Children In Need
30. Lalla Ward

31. The Spiridons
32. Scaroth
33. Arbitan
34. Paradise Towers
35. *Snakedance*
36. Madeleine Issigri
37. The Vardans, The Sontarans
38. Adric
39. Peter Sallis
40. A magic bandage

41. Aggedor
42. Doctor Who
43. Lexa
44. Chumblies
45. Red
46. Crawford
47. Patrick Troughton
48. Russell T Davies
49. Axonite
50. *The Ambassadors of Death*

QUIZ 3

1. Lazar
2. Cyanide
3. The third
4. The Master
5. Patrick Troughton
6. *K-9 and Company*
7. Drashigs
8. Manussa
9. The audio log
10. Jovanka

11. Damos
12. Italy
13. Shur
14. The Sontarans
15. Movellan Virus
16. Thunderbolt missile
17. Metebelis 3
18. John Cleese
19. *The Celestial Toymaker*
20. Doctor Who

21. Morgaine
22. Grace Holloway and Chang Lee

23. *Time and the Rani*
24. Dorothy
25. The Gravitron
26. Chameleon Tours
27. Mestor
28. Desperus
29. *The Doctor*
30. The Cybermen

31. The BOSS
32. The Foamasi
33. Sarah Jane Smith
34. *Survival*
35. Mickey
36. The Ultima Machine
37. Irongron
38. *Marco Polo*
39. They turn into a Varga plant
40. Devesham

41. Vislor Turlough
42. *The Underwater Menace*
43. Mr Sin
44. K-1
45. Segonax
46. Richard Briers
47. The title music
48. *The Mind Robber*
49. The Drahvins
50. Greel's Lair

QUIZ 4

1. Time and Relative Dimensions In Space
2. A Sea Devil
3. Theta, Gamma
4. Ace
5. The sonic screwdriver
6. Sir George Hutchinson
7. False
8. True
9. Calufrax
10. Andromeda

11. *The Book of the Old Time*
12. *The Arc of Infinity*
13. Alpha Centauri
14. *Logopolis*
15. Ian Chesterton and Barbara Wright
16. Count Grendel
17. *Robot*
18. Scotland
19. Jo Grant
20. Fifi

21. The Beta Buccaneer
22. The second Doctor
23. Tom Baker
24. *Delta and the Bannermen*
25. Jamie
26. Geneva
27. 10 beats per minute
28. Peter Davison
29. Professor Stahlman
30. 1,000 years

31. Once every 50 years
32. Xeros
33. Jugglebox
34. The fifth
35. Xeros
36. *The Three Doctors*

37. Using an umbrella in the rain
38. Miss Hawthorne
39. *Genesis of the Daleks*
40. Dot Cotton

41. The Vanir
42. Katarina
43. A metal
44. Windsor
45. Slaar
46. Light and Control
47. A satellite
48. *Remembrance of the Daleks*
49. Davros
50. *The Curse of Fenric*

QUIZ 5

1. David Tennant
2. Rose Tyler
3. One
4. A glowing ball they hold
5. K9
6. The UN
7. Lady Cassandra
8. Jackie Tyler
9. The Preachers
10. Elton Pope

11. Satellite 5
12. The 2012 Olympic Games
13. 900 years old
14. *The Weakest Link*
15. 10 Downing Street
16. Mauve
17. Ricky

18. Tommy
19. Jefferson
20. A gas mask

21. Bad Wolf
22. Utah
23. London
24. Chip's body
25. Mr Sneed
26. The Gelth
27. A pig
28. Cybus Industries
29. Mickey Smith
30. Rose

31. The Editor
32. A wedding
33. Father Angelo
34. Anne Droid
35. Alexandra Palace
36. John Jefferson
37. Catherine Tate
38. The Scasis Paradigm
39. Captain Jack Harkness
40. The Ood

41. A Volkswagen Beetle
42. Scotland
43. Humans
44. His hand
45. Detective Inspector Bishop, Tommy Connolly
46. Bronze medal
47. Psychic paper
48. The Golden Locust
49. Barcelona
50. 1,600 credits

QUIZ 6

1. 5,000
2. Jo Grant
3. Frogs
4. Peter Davison
5. Exxilon
6. Professor Zaroff
7. The Emperor Dalek
8. Professor Brett
9. A circle of mirrors
10. His leg

11. Tullock
12. The Sontarans
13. True
14. Davros
15. Cybermen
16. Tegan
17. *The Gunfighters*
18. Paul Darrow
19. Edward Waterfield
20. Dinosaurs

21. The Visians
22. The Cybermen
23. Marine Space Corps
24. The Time Lords
25. Number 9
26. Professor Clifford Jones
27. Mechanoids
28. The Daleks
29. Tegan's
30. Florana

31. Zoe Heriot
32. *The Macra Terror*
33. The Master

34. Heathrow airport
35. Colin Baker
36. *The Clangers*
37. Peru
38. *Destiny of the Daleks*
39. See what they most fear
40. UNIT

41. The fourth Doctor
42. Six
43. Johnny Ringo
44. Wales
45. Chancellor Goth
46. The Nine Travellers group of standing stones
47. The Zarbi
48. Kassia
49. Coal Hill School
50. The Conscience Machine

QUIZ 7

1. Atlantis
2. Professor Zaroff
3. *Destiny of the Daleks*
4. Omega
5. *Arc of Infinity*
6. Mars
7. *Spearhead from Space*
8. False
9. Science Officer O'Connor
10. The Doctor's scarf

11. *The Green Death*
12. *Fury from the Deep*
13. Colin Baker
14. Sutekh
15. Tegana

16. The Doctor
17. Jon Pertwee
18. 1989
19. Brian Cant
20. The Master

21. Jondar, Areta
22. Nyssa
23. Gallifrey
24. The Daleks
25. Count Scarlioni
26. Wales
27. John Cleese, Eleanor Bron
28. Bendalypse
29. The Thals
30. Ogri

31. Ben and Polly
32. *The Moonbase*
33. Nimrod
34. The Rani's
35. Azal
36. The swimming pool
37. *The Time Meddler*
38. Jim Troughton
39. Red
40. The second Doctor

41. The TARDIS
42. Three
43. The Time Lords
44. Control
45. The Master
46. The Master
47. The Land of Fiction
48. Jason Connery
49. *Snakedance*

50. Earth

QUIZ 8

1. Mechanus
2. A yo-yo
3. *Genesis of the Daleks*
4. 450 years old
5. General Cutler's son
6. The Rutan
7. Sara Kingdom
8. Pex
9. Nils
10. Professor Kettlewell

11. David Troughton
12. His granddaughter
13. False (she was the companion in *Doctor Who: The Movie*)
14. *The Abominable Snowmen*
15. Eric Klieg, Kaftan
16. Romulus, Remus
17. Doctor Who
18. Insects
19. Silver
20. Adric, Nyssa and Tegan Jovanka

21. Za
22. Sonic screwdriver
23. Six
24. The Mona Lisa
25. The Inquisitor
26. The first Doctor
27. William Hartnell
28. Iceworld

29. Tom Baker
30. Professor Zaroff

31. Marinus
32. Australian
33. The Krynoid
34. World War II
35. The Chameleons
36. 12
37. Pangol
38. Romana (Mark I)
39. The third Doctor
40. Jodrell Bank

41. A triceratops
42. White
43. Mars
44. The Mechanoids
45. Light
46. Professor Arthur Stengos
47. Lucy
48. Vampires
49. 1979
50. *Remembrance of the Daleks*

QUIZ 9

1. The Island of Death
2. *Power of the Daleks*
3. Sam Seeley
4. Camilla, Aukon and Zargo
5. Sergeant Benton
6. United Nations Intelligence Taskforce
7. Concorde
8. Supreme Dalek
9. The Master

10. International Space Command
11. Bok
12. Z-bomb
13. Union Jacks
14. Dodo
15. The Scientific Reform Society
16. The second Doctor
17. Voga
18. A washerwoman, a British soldier
19. The Daleks
20. *Spearhead from Space*

21. Dodo Chaplet's
22. Jon Pertwee
23. Gaztaks
24. Harrison Chase
25. The English Civil War
26. *City of Death*
27. Cybermats
28. Magnus Greel
29. *Terror of the Autons*
30. The Fendahl

31. Tom Baker and Sylvester McCoy
32. Madame Tussaud's
33. The Sisterhood of Karn
34. Doris
35. Valentine Dyall
36. Sonic screwdriver
37. 1963
38. *The Mind Robber*
39. The Daleks
40. SIDRATs

41. Gilbert M
42. The Daleks
43. Celery
44. Purple
45. Alf Roberts
46. Major General Scobie
47. Mr Stimson
48. *The War Games*
49. Patrick Troughton
50. Mondas

QUIZ 10

1. Princess Astra
2. *The Chase*
3. The tree
4. A secret society
5. Patrick Troughton
6. Chessene
7. *Whodunnit?*
8. A stethoscope
9. A question mark
10. Global Chemicals

11. His left eye
12. Refusis II
13. Voga
14. London
15. Three
16. Atrios and Zeos
17. Dryfoots
18. Magnus Greel
19. The Toymaker's
20. *The Edge of Destruction*

21. Kara
22. Thous
23. Princess Astra

24. Vicki
25. *The Tomb of the Cybermen*
26. Belladonna
27. Autons
28. The Kralls
29. Suns
30. Colonel

31. Professor Brett, Auxon
32. Hostile Action Displacement System
33. Senta
34. The Rani
35. Ribos
36. Eldrad
37. Sarah Jane Smith
38. Loch Ness
39. Geneva
40. The first Doctor

41. False (he is immortal)
42. New South Wales
43. *The Web Planet*
44. Katarina
45. *The Sea Devils*
46. Refusis II
47. *The Sun Makers*
48. *The Stones of Blood*
49. The Wirrn
50. Rassilon

QUIZ 11

1. David Tennant
2. Electric Light Orchestra (ELO)

3. Rose
4. Queen Victoria
5. 'The bitter pill'
6. The Daleks
7. Mickey Smith
8. Harriet Jones
9. Dinner lady
10. His mummy

11. Betamax video cassette
12. Suki
13. The Earth
14. Captain Jack Harkness
15. 10 miles
16. Cybermen
17. Klom
18. Her passport
19. A hit and run accident
20. Sarah Jane Smith

21. The North Sea
22. The Sycorax
23. Graphite
24. Making a cocktail
25. Rose
26. *Bad Wolf*
27. Earth
28. Rats
29. New New York
30. The Prime Minister

31. A Dalek
32. 100 credits
33. The head (forehead)
34. Mickey Smith's computer
35. Mickey
36. Victor Kennedy

37. Toby
38. *The End of the World*
39. Albion Hospital
40. Lynda Moss

41. Torchwood Tower
42. Magpie
43. A-positive
44. Grandad Prentice
45. The Moxx of Balhoon
46. Blaidd Drwg
47. Cardiff
48. Freema Agyeman
49. Number 3
50. Shayne Ward

QUIZ 12

1. The Shangri-La Holiday Camp
2. Victoria
3. The North Sea
4. Varos
5. The Lake of Mutations
6. 500 years
7. Skarasen
8. The SS Bernice
9. The sixth Doctor
10. London Underground

11. Xoanon
12. The Doctor's
13. Peri
14. *The Wheel*
15. Chef
16. The Black Albatross
17. Peter Purves
18. Romana (mark II)

19. *The Pyramids of Mars*
20. 100,000 years

21. The Greeks
22. Robomen
23. Autloc
24. *Spearhead from Space*
25. The Space Security Department
26. Quarks
27. Giant Maggots
28. The Master
29. *The Highlanders*
30. Sydney

31. Squash
32. Lord Ravensworth
33. The Daleks
34. The Trilogic Game
35. Pink
36. Drax
37. Mena
38. *Castrovalva*
39. Chang Lee
40. Queen Huath

41. Two
42. Kenneth Kendal
43. The Cybermen
44. The Voord
45. Jo Grant
46. Blue
47. The Amazon
48. Barbara
49. Androzani Minor
50. The Daleks

QUIZ 13

1. The Time Destructor
2. Leonardo da Vinci
3. Napoleon
4. His brother
5. Zoe Heriot
6. Solar energy
7. Grace Holloway
8. Mavic Chen
9. *The Romans*
10. Councillor Hedin

11. The Royal Air Force (RAF)
12. Terra Alpha
13. Gallifrey
14. Two hearts
15. Steven Taylor
16. Professor Brett
17. White
18. Tony Hancock
19. Astra
20. Fish People

21. Jarvis Bennett
22. Gold
23. *Arrangements for War*
24. Tegan
25. *Enlightenment*
26. The Daleks
27. *The War Games*
28. Doctor Caligari
29. A science teacher
30. The Voords

31. Torbis
32. A bird
33. *The Two Doctors*

34. Valeyard
35. Jon Pertwee
36. Colonel Faraday
37. The Governor
38. Queen Xanxia
39. Poul
40. *The Massacre*

41. DN6
42. Lytton
43. The Nut Hutch
44. Morbius
45. Jano
46. Adelaide
47. Kane
48. Ben Jackson
49. *Battlefield*
50. Two

QUIZ 14

1. The Master
2. *The War Games*
3. Adric, Nyssa
4. Navarinos
5. His hands
6. An ultra-violet converter
7. Susan Foreman
8. The Cybermen
9. Alexei Sayle
10. Sarah Jane Smith

11. Patrick Troughton
12. Giant Maggots
13. Tranquil Repose
14. His vintage car
15. Taren Capel

16. The first Doctor
17. A statue
18. A chauffeur
19. *Silver Nemesis*
20. Morton Dill

21. Salamander
22. The sixth
23. The Plain of Stones
24. *The King's Demons and Planet of Fire*
25. *The Gunfighters*
26. 144 mirrors
27. Melanie Bush
28. The planet Xeros
29. The Black Guardian
30. A wheelchair

31. Professor Sorenson
32. Green
33. Mel (Melanie Bush)
34. Earth (in the far distant future)
35. The Yeti
36. Mira
37. The Bi-Al Foundation
38. Bessie
39. The Deadly Assassin
40. Validium

41. A tree
42. The Moon
43. Daffodils
44. Sharaz Jek
45. *The Happiness Patrol*
46. Thals
47. Harrison Chase
48. Dido

49. Red
50. An explosive

QUIZ 15

1. Professor
2. Ace
3. Venusian aikido
4. *The Talons of Weng-Chiang*
5. *The Wheel in Space*
6. The Silurians
7. False
8. Solon
9. Stone
10. 3,000 years

11. Terra Alpha
12. His right hand
13. *Shada*
14. Salamander
15. Peladon
16. HG Wells
17. Houdini
18. *Black Orchid*
19. The Daleks
20. Nyssa

21. Tegan
22. Three
23. The Krotons
24. Spain
25. Kal
26. *The Android Invasion*
27. Gangs of girls
28. Sixth Doctor
29. Cyril
30. Terminus

31. Noah
32. The Rani
33. Varsh
34. Salt
35. A rocking horse
36. The Doctor
37. A form of travel
38. The first Doctor
39. Polly Wright
40. The fifth Doctor

41. True
42. The Time Lords
43. Green
44. *Power of the Daleks*
45. *The Stones of Blood*
46. Barbara
47. Nyssa
48. Sabalom Glitz
49. £5,000
50. Exit

QUIZ 16

1. Dodo
2. Gold
3. Jo Grant
4. Andred
5. Diamonds
6. 'Holy' Joe Longfoot
7. Steven Taylor
8. The Master's
9. Four
10. The Doctor

11. Earth
12. The Keeper of Traken
13. The 1930s

14. Sarn
15. Adric
16. Republican Security Forces
17. Tutor
18. Twelfth
19. Blue
20. The Master

21. A skull
22. The K-1 robot
23. Ian Chesterton
24. The Pipe People
25. Salamander
26. Jacqueline Pearce
27. Zoe
28. *The League of Gentlemen*
29. De Flores
30. Yellow

31. Colin Baker
32. Five times – *The Ambassadors of Death, The Seeds of Death, The Green Death, Death to the Daleks, City of Death*
33. Helium
34. Tegan
35. Monoids
36. A computer
37. Psychic Circus
38. Sarah Greene
39. Meteorites
40. False

41. Sara Kingdom
42. Ky

43. General Cutler
44. Run a secondhand car dealership
45. Pluto
46. *The Tale of Peter Rabbit*
47. A tuning fork
48. Patrick Troughton
49. International Electromatics
50. Alzarius

QUIZ 17

1. Christopher Eccleston
2. Torchwood
3. One
4. Mickey Smith
5. Captain Jack Harkness
6. Mistletoe
7. Big Ben
8. Mickey Smith
9. The Duke of Manhattan
10. The Olympic torch

11. Charles Dickens
12. His cane
13. Jabe
14. The Powell Estate
15. Room 802
16. Mars
17. A Metaltron
18. Flora
19. Jackie Tyler
20. Sonic Screwdriver

21. A Dalek
22. Lime Street
23. A motor scooter

24. A telescope
25. Nancy
26. Five million
27. The eyepiece
28. Rose
29. Rose
30. Margaret Blaine

31. *The Signalman*
32. Ursula Blake
33. Ida
34. The Torchwood Institute
35. Milo
36. 'Master'
37. Mr Redpath's
38. A horse
39. Wilson
40. Chloe Webber

41. 7.30 am
42. Jackie
43. Fitch
44. Lady Cassandra
45. Crosbie
46. Five billion years
47. Clive
48. Trisha Delaney
49. Eva Saint Julienne
50. 'Tainted Love' by Soft Cell

QUIZ 18

1. Leela
2. Greg Sutton
3. Gate, organ, cabinet
4. The Thals
5. Uranus
6. The Master's

7. Jo Grant
8. Sabalom Glitz
9. Amdo
10. Douglas Adams

11. Suzanne Danielle
12. The seventh Doctor
13. *The Time Monster*
14. Four
15. To heal after regeneration
16. Peri
17. JK Rowling
18. The Marshmen
19. Cybermen
20. William Hartnell

21. Sylvester McCoy
22. A grandfather clock
23. *Bridge Over The River Kwai*
24. The Master
25. The Borad
26. Gallifrey
27. Metal
28. Sarah Jane Smith
29. Two
30. Ace

31. *Hamlet*
32. Empress and Hecate
33. Supreme Controller
34. The Tissue Compression Eliminator
35. *The Seeds of Doom*
36. Yrcanos
37. Drowning
38. Chal

39. Shockeye
40. Ian Chesterton

41. The third Doctor
42. Horus
43. Sylvester McCoy
44. Graff
45. Milo Clancey
46. The Monk's
47. Polly
48. Dodo Chaplet
49. An ambulance
50. Morgaine

QUIZ 19

1. Black
2. The Time Lords
3. Three
4. An egg
5. Gwyneth
6. Scooter
7. *New Earth*
8. A banana grove
9. Cardiff
10. Psychic paper

11. Adam
12. The Face of Boe
13. Eddie Connolly
14. A church
15. Danny Llewellyn
16. Medicine
17. Gas
18. Rose's father
19. President John F. Kennedy

20. Japan

21. A Chula spaceship
22. Jackie Tyler
23. Harriet Jones
24. *'The Oncoming Storm'*
25. EastEnders
26. A photo of Rose
27. In the road (underneath the tarmac)
28. A fire extinguisher
29. Lady Cassandra
30. Henry van Statten's

31. Three days
32. The Wire
33. The Ood
34. LINDA
35. Norway
36. Mr Finch
37. Captain Jack Harkness
38. 12 months
39. Spiders
40. Deffry Vale High School

41. Henrik's
42. Louis XV
43. The Blockheads
44. Gwyneth
45. Buffalo
46. A Kronkburger
47. Strategy nine
48. Bad Wolf Bay
49. RLF 771R
50. 'Don't Bring Me Down'

DIFFICULT QUIZ

1. Totters Lane
2. Romanadvoratrelundar
3. Vionesium
4. Two circular discs
5. Wallscrawl
6. Captain Cook
7. Bimorphic Operational Systems Supervisor
8. Theta Sigma
9. Hi Fi
10. *City of Death* and *The Robots of Death*

11. British Institute of Druidic Studies
12. Marriner
13. Morgus
14. God Rest Ye, Merry Gentlemen
15. Lavinia Smith
16. Eats the vegetable
17. Will Operating Thought Analogue
18. Continuous Event Transmuter
19. Sergeant Benton
20. Captain Wrack

21. *Survival*
22. Demeter
23. The mouth of the carving of the Doctor's face
24. Sir James Gregson

25. Jack Ringwood
26. Ichtar
27. Six inches
28. Skonnos
29. Deadbeat
30. Firestorm

31. Inter Minor
32. Neurotrope X
33. Cybermats
34. Harry Slocum
35. Ta
36. Four (three crew plus the civilian, Kellman)
37. Human beings
38. Metropolitan
39. Linx
40. Chancellor Goth

41. The Doctor Who Appreciation Society convention
42. The Nine Travellers
43. The Tractators
44. The Raston Warrior Robot
45. Loman
46. Brigadier Winnifred Bambera
47. Trevor Sigma
48. Ray (Rachel)
49. Transmission of Matter Through Interstitial Time
50. NF3226